EGYPTIAN MYTHS
AND
MYSTERIES

EGYPTIAN MYTHS
AND
MYSTERIES

Twelve Lectures
by
RUDOLF STEINER

Leipzig, September 2–14, 1908

ANTHROPOSOPHIC PRESS, INC.
NEW YORK

Translated from shorthand reports un-
revised by the lecturer, from the German edition published with the title,
Aegyptische Mythen und Mysterien
(Vol. 106 in the *Bibliographical Survey*, 1961). Translated by Norman
Macbeth.

This translation has been authorized
for the Western Hemisphere by the
Rudolf Steiner Nachlassverwaltung,
Dornach, Switzerland.

Printed in the United States of America

CONTENTS

EGYPTIAN MYTHS
AND
MYSTERIES

LECTURE 1

*Spiritual Connections between
the Culture-streams of Ancient
and Modern Times.*

September 2, 1908

IF we ask ourselves what spiritual science should be for men, then presumably, out of all sorts of reactions and feelings that we have developed in the course of our work in this field, we will place the following answer before our souls: Spiritual science should be for us a path to the higher development of our humanity, of all that is human in us.

Thus we set up a life-aim, which in a certain way is self-understood for every thinking and feeling person, a life-aim that includes the achieving of the highest ideals and also includes the unfolding of the deepest and most significant forces in our souls. The best men in all ages have asked themselves how man can rightly bring to expression what lies within him, and to this question the most diverse answers have been given. Perhaps none can be found that is terser or more telling than the answer Goethe gave out of a deep conviction in his *Geheimnisse*:

1

"From the power that binds all beings
That man frees himself who overcomes himself."

Deep meaning lies in these words, for they show us clearly and pregnantly what lies at the heart of all evolution. This is that man develops his inner feeling through rising above himself. Thereby we lift ourselves, so to speak, above ourselves. The soul that overcomes itself finds the path that leads beyond itself to the highest treasures of humanity. This lofty goal of spiritual research should be borne in mind when we undertake to treat such a theme as the one that is to occupy us here. It will lead us beyond the ordinary horizons of life to sublime things. We will have to survey wide reaches of time if we take as our subject an epoch stretching from ancient Egypt down to our own day. We will have to pass millennia in review, and what we gain therefrom will really be something connected with the deepest concerns of our souls, something that grips our innermost soul-life. Only apparently does the man who strives toward the heights of life remove himself from his immediate surroundings; just through this he comes to an understanding of his daily concerns. Man must get away from the troubles of the day, from what his routine brings to him, and look up to the great events of the history of the world and its peoples. Then for the first time he finds what is most sacred for his soul. It may seem strange to suggest that connections, intimate connections, should be sought for between our own time and ancient Egypt, when the mighty pyramids and the Sphinx appeared. It can at first seem remarkable that one should understand his own time better by directing his gaze so far back. But just for this purpose we are going to look backward over much wider and more comprehensive epochs. This will bring the result we seek: The possibility of transcending ourselves.

To one who has already carefully studied the ideas of spiritual science, it will not seem strange that one should look for a connection between widely separated periods of time. It is one of our basic convictions that the human soul continually returns, that the experiences between birth and death occur repeatedly for us. The doctrine of reincarnation has become ever more familiar to us. When we reflect on this we may ask: Since these souls that dwell in us today have often been here before, is it not possible that they were also present in ancient Egypt during the Egyptian cultural epoch, that the same souls are in us which at that time looked up at the gigantic pyramids and the enigmatic sphinxes?

The answer to this question is, Yes. Our souls have beheld the old cultural monuments that they see again today. The same souls that lived then have gone through later periods and have appeared again in our own time. We know that no life remains without fruit; we know that what the soul has gone through in the way of experiences remains within it and appears in later incarnations as powers, temperament, capacities, and dispositions. Thus the way we look on nature today, the way we take up what our times bring forth, the way we view the world, all this was prepared in ancient Egypt, in the land of the pyramids. We were then prepared in such a way that we now look at the physical world as we do. Just how these widely separated periods link themselves together is what we will now explore.

If we want to grasp the deeper meaning of these lectures, we must go a long way back in earthly evolution. We know that our earth has often changed. Before ancient Egypt there were still other cultures. By means of occult research we can see much further back into the gray primeval times of human evolution, and we come to times when the earth appeared quite other than it is today. Things were entirely different in ancient Asia and Africa. If we look back clairvoyantly into primeval times, we come to a point where a tremendous catastrophe, caused by water-forces, took place on our earth and fundamentally altered its face. If we go still further back, we reach a time when the earth had an entirely different physiognomy, when what now forms the floor of the Atlantic Ocean, between Europe and America, was above water, was land. We come to a time when our souls lived in entirely different bodies than today; we reach

3

ancient Atlantis, of which our external science can as yet say little.

The regions of Atlantis were destroyed through colossal deluges. Human bodies had different forms at that time, but the souls that live in us today lived also in the ancient Atlanteans. Those were our souls. Then the water-catastrophe caused a movement of the Atlantean peoples, a great migration from west to east. We ourselves were these peoples. Toward the end of Atlantis all was in movement. We wandered from the west toward the east, through Ireland, Scotland, Holland, France, and Spain. Thus the peoples moved eastward and populated Europe, Asia, and the northern parts of Africa.

It must not be imagined that those who, in the last great migration, wandered out of the west into the regions that have gradually developed into Asia, Europe, and Africa, did not encounter other peoples. Almost all of Europe, the northern parts of Africa, and large parts of Asia were already inhabited at that time. These areas were not peopled from the west only; they had already been settled earlier, so that this migration found a strange population already established. We may assume that when quieter times set in, special cultural relations arose. There was, for instance, in the neighborhood of Ireland, a region where, before the catastrophe that now lies thousands of years behind us, there lived the most advanced portions of the entire population of the earth. These portions then migrated, under the special guidance of great individualities, through Europe to a region of central Asia, and from that point cultural colonies were sent out to the most diverse places. One such colony of the post-Atlantean time was sent from this group of people into India, finding a population that had been seated there from primeval times and had its own culture. Paying due heed to what was already present, these colonists founded the first post-Atlantean culture. This was many thousand years ago, and external documents tell us scarcely anything about it. What appears in these documents is much later. In those great compendiums of wisdom called the Vedas, we have only the final echoes of a very early Indian culture that

4

was directed by super-earthly beings and was founded by the Holy Rishis. It was a culture of a unique kind, and we today can form only a feeble idea of it because the Vedas are only a reflection of that primeval holy Indian culture.

After this culture there followed another, the second cultural epoch of the post-Atlantean time. Out of this the wisdom of Zarathustra flowed and the Persian culture arose. Long did the Indian culture endure, long also the Persian, reaching a culmination in Zarathustra.

Then arose, under the influence of colonists who were sent into the land of the Nile, the culture that is comprised under the four names, Chaldean-Egyptian-Assyrian-Babylonian. This third post-Atlantean culture in Asia Minor and northern Africa, and reached its summit, on the one side, in the wonderful Chaldean star-lore and, on the other, in the Egyptian culture.

Then comes a fourth age, developing in the south of Europe, the age of the Greco-Roman culture, which dawns with the songs of Homer and goes on to produce the Greek sculptures and the art of poetry that appears in the tragedies of Aeschylus and Sophocles. Rome also belonged to this period. The epoch begins in the eighth pre-Christian century, approximately in 747 B. C., and lasts until the fourteenth or fifteenth century A. D. After that we have the fifth period, in which we ourselves live, and this in turn will be followed by the sixth and seventh periods.

In the seventh period, ancient India will appear in a new form. We shall see that there is a remarkable law that enables us to understand the working of wonderful forces through the various epochs and the relationships of the epochs to each other. If we begin by looking at the first period, that of the Indian culture, we will find that this first culture later recrudesces in a new form in the seventh period. Ancient India will then appear in a new form. Mysterious forces are at work here. And the second period, which we have called the Persian, will appear again in the sixth period. After our own culture perishes, we will see the Zarathustra religion revive in the culture of the sixth period. And in the course of these lectures we will see how, in our own fifth period,

5

there takes place a sort of reawakening of the third period, the Egyptian. The fourth period stands in the middle; it is peculiar to itself, and neither earlier nor later does it have a parallel.

To make this mysterious law somewhat clearer, we should add the following. We know that India has something that strikes our humanitarian consciousness as strange. This is the division into definite castes, into priests, warriors, merchants, and laborers. This strict segregation is foreign to our modern views. In the first post-Atlantean culture it was not strange, it was entirely natural; in those times it could not be otherwise than that the souls of men should be divided into four grades according to their capacities. No harshness was felt in it for men were distributed by their leaders, who had such authority that what they prescribed was accepted without question. It was felt that the leaders, the seven Holy Rishis who had received their instruction from divine beings in Atlantis, could see where each man should be placed. Thus such a classification of men was something altogether natural. An entirely different grouping will appear in the seventh period. The division in the first period was effected by authority, but in the seventh period men will group themselves according to objective points of view. Something similar is seen among the ants; they form a state which, in its wonderful structure as well as in its capacity to perform a relatively prodigious amount of work, is not rivaled by any human state. Yet there we have just what seems to be alien to us, the caste system; for each ant has its particular task.

Whatever we may think of this today, men will see that the salvation of humanity lies in division into objective groups, and they will even be able to combine division of labor with equality of rights. Human society will appear as a wonderful harmony. This is something we can see in the annals of the future. Thus ancient India will appear again; and in a similar way certain traits of the third period will appear again in the fifth.

Glancing at the immediate implications of our theme, we see a large domain. We see the gigantic pyramids, the enigmatic Sphinx. The souls that belonged to the ancient Indians were also

6

incarnated in Egypt and are again incarnated today. If we follow our general line of thought into detail, we will discover two phenomena that show us how, in *superearthly* connections, there are mysterious threads between the Egyptian culture and that of today. We have observed the law of repetition in the different periods of time, but it will seem far more significant if we follow it in spiritual regions. We are all familiar with a painting of great importance that has surely passed before all our souls at least once. I mean Raphael's famous painting of the Sistine Madonna, which by a chain of circumstances has come to be located among us in central Germany. In this picture, which is available in countless reproductions, we have learned to admire the wonderful purity poured out over the whole form. We have all felt something in the countenance of the mother, in the singular way the form floats in the air, perhaps also in the deep expression of the child's eyes. Then, if we see the cloudforms round about from which numerous little angel-heads appear, we have a still deeper feeling, a feeling that makes the whole picture more comprehensible to us. I know it seems daring when I say that if one gazes deeply and earnestly on this child in the arms of the mother and on the clouds in the background forming themselves into a number of little angel-heads, then he has the feeling that this child was not born in the natural way, but that it is one of those that float round about in the clouds. This Jesus child itself is such a cloud-form, only become a little denser, as though one of the little angels had flown out of the clouds onto the arm of the Madonna. That would be a healthy feeling. If we make this feeling live within us, then our view will expand and free itself from certain narrow conceptions about the natural connections of life. Just out of such a picture our narrow vision can be expanded to see that what must happen in a certain way according to modern laws could at one time have been different. We will discern that there was once a form of reproduction other than the sexual one. In short, we will perceive deep connections between what is human and the spiritual forces in this picture. This is what lies in it.

7

If we allow our gaze to wander back from this Madonna into the Egyptian time, we are met by something similar, by an equally sublime picture. The Egyptian had Isis, the figure connected with the words: *I am what was, what is, and what will be. No mortal has yet raised my veil.*

A deep mystery, heavily veiled, manifests itself in the figure of Isis, the lovable goddess who, in the spiritual consciousness of the ancient Egyptian, was present with the Horus child as our Madonna is present today with the Jesus child. In the fact that this Isis is presented to us as something bearing the eternal within it, we are again reminded of our feeling in contemplating the Madonna. We must see deep mysteries in Isis, mysteries that are grounded in the spiritual. The Madonna is a remembrance of Isis: Isis appears again in the Madonna. This is one of the connections that I spoke of. We must learn to recognize with our feelings the deep mysteries that show a superearthly connection between ancient Egypt and our modern culture.

Still another connection can be brought before you today. We recall how the Egyptian handled the dead; we remember the mummies, and how the Egyptian concerned himself that the outer physical form should be preserved for a long time. We know that he filled his tombs with such mummies, in which he had preserved the outer form, and that as mementoes of the past physical life he gave to the deceased certain utensils and possessions suited to the needs of physical life. Thus what the person had had in the physical was to be retained. In this way the Egyptian bound the dead to the physical plane. This custom developed more and more and is a special earmark of the old Egyptian culture. Such a thing is not without consequences for the soul. Let us remember that our souls were in Egyptian bodies. This is quite correct; our souls were incorporated in these bodies that became mummies. We know that when man, after death, is freed from his physical and etheric bodies, he has a different consciousness; he is by no means unconscious in the astral world. He can look down from the spiritual world, even though today he cannot look up; he can then look down on the physical earth.

It is not then indifferent to him whether his body has been preserved as a mummy, has been burned, or has decayed. A definite kind of connection arises through this. We shall see this mysterious connection. Through the fact that in ancient Egypt the bodies were preserved for a long time, the souls experienced something very definite in the period after death. When they looked down they knew—that is my body. They were bound to this physical body. They had the form of their body before them. This body became important to the souls, for the soul is susceptible to impressions after death. The impression made by the mummified body imprinted itself deeply, and the soul was formed in accordance with this impression.

These souls went through incarnations in the Greco-Latin period, and in our own time they are living in us. It was not without effect that they saw their mummified bodies after death, that they were repeatedly led back to these bodies; this is by no means unimportant. They attached their sympathies to these bodies, and the fruit of their looking down upon them appears now, in the fifth period, in the inclination that souls have today to lay great weight upon the outer physical life. All that we describe today as the attachment to matter stems from the fact that the souls at that time, out of the spiritual world, could look upon their own embodiment. Through this man learned to love the physical world; through this it is so often said today that the only important thing is the physical body between birth and death. Such views do not arise out of nothing.

This is not a criticism of the practice of mummifying. We only want to point to certain necessities that are connected with the repeated incarnating of the soul. Without this pondering on the mummies men would not have been equal to developing further. We would by now have lost all interest in the physical world had the Egyptians not had the mummy-cult. It had to be thus if a proper interest in the physical world was to be awakened. That we see the world as we do today is a consequence of the fact that the Egyptians mummified the physical body after death.

This cultural stream was under the influence of initiates, who

9

could see into the future. Not through any whim did men make mummies. Particularly in those days mankind was led by high individualities who prescribed what was right. This was done under authority. In the schools of the initiates it was known that our fifth epoch was connected with the third epoch. These mysterious connections stood at that time before the eyes of the priests, who instituted mummification so that the souls might acquire the disposition to seek spiritual experience in the external physical world.

The world is guided through wisdom; this is a second example of such connections. That men think as they do today is a result of what they experienced in ancient Egypt. Here we glimpse deep mysteries that reveal themselves in the cultural streams. We have barely touched these mysteries, for what has been shown of the Madonna as a remembrance of Isis, together with what we have seen of mummification, gives only a feeble hint of the real spiritual connections. But we will throw more light upon these relationships; we will consider not only what appears outwardly, but also what lies behind the external.

External life runs its course between birth and death. Man lives a much longer life after death, in what we know as kamaloka and the experiences of the spiritual world. The experiences in the supersensible worlds are no more uniform than the experiences here in the physical world. What did we experience as ancient Egyptians in the other world?

When our eyes looked on the pyramids and the Sphinx, how completely different was the course of our lives, how differently did our souls live between birth and death! That life cannot be compared to the life of the present day; such a comparison would have no meaning, and the experiences between death and a new birth have been far more dissimilar than the experiences of outer life. During the Egyptian epoch the soul experienced something quite different than in the Greek world, or in the time of Charlemagne, or in our own time. Also in the other world, in the spiritual world, evolution takes place, and what the soul experiences today between death and a new birth is something quite different from what the ancient Egyptian experienced when he laid aside his outer form at death. Just as mummification worked on in its peculiar way, causing the mood of the present day, just as this external life repeats itself from the third into the fifth period, so does evolution continue in those mysterious worlds between death and birth. This also we will have to study and here again we will find a mysterious connection. Then we will be able to grasp what lives in us as the fruit of that ancient time. We will be led into deep recesses of the labyrinth of the earth's evolution. But just through this we will recognize the full connection between what the Egyptian built, what the Chaldean thought, and what we today live. We will see what was then achieved flaring up again in what surrounds us, in what interests us in our environment. Physically and spiritually we will obtain clues to this connection. It will also be shown how evolution proceeds, how the fourth period forms a wonderful link between the third and the fifth. Thus our souls will lift themselves to the significant connections of the world, and the fruit will be a deep understanding of what lives in us.

LECTURE 2

The Reflection of Cosmic Events in the Religious Views of Men.

September 3, 1908

YESTERDAY we looked at certain connections in the spiritual relationships of the so-called post-Atlantean time. We saw how the first cultural epoch of this period will repeat itself in the last, the seventh; how the Persian culture will repeat itself in the sixth; and how the Egyptian culture, which will occupy us during the next few days, repeats itself in our own lives and destinies in the fifth period. Of the fourth culture, the Greco-Latin, we were able to say that it occupies an exceptional position in that it experiences no repetition. Thus we could point in a sketchy way to the mysterious connections in the cultures of the post-Atlantean time, which follows after the time of the Atlantis that perished through powerful water-catastrophes. This age that follows Atlantis will perish in turn. At the end of our fifth great epoch, the post-Atlantean, there will be catastrophes that will work in a way similar to those at the close of the Atlantean epoch. Through the War of All Against All, the seventh culture of the fifth epoch will find its conclusion. These are interesting connections that are indicated in certain repetitions, and when we follow them more closely they will throw light into the depths of our soul life.

In order to lay a proper foundation, we must today allow still other repetitions to pass before our mind's eye. We will let our glance rove far into the evolution of our earth, and we will see that these wide horizons must have an intimate interest for us.

But let us begin with an admonition, a warning against a mechanical approach to the repetitions. When in the realm of occultism we speak of such repetitions, saying that the first cultural epoch repeats itself in the seventh, the third in the fifth, etc., it is easy to let a certain gift for combinations get the upper hand, so that we try to apply such schemes or diagrams in other contexts also. It is easy to believe that we can do this, and many books on theosophy actually contain a good deal of rubbish of this sort. Hence there must be a strong warning that such combinations are not controlling, but only perception, spiritual vision, without which we go astray. Such combinations must be warned against. What we can read in the spiritual world may be understood, but not discovered, through logic. It can be discovered only through experience.

If we wish to understand the cultural epochs more clearly, we must achieve a general view of the evolution of the earth as it presents itself to the seer who can direct his spiritual gaze to the events of the most remote past. If we look far back into the evolution of the earth, we can say that our earth has not always appeared as it does today. It did not have the firm mineral base of today; the mineral kingdom was not as it is today; the earth did not bear the same plants and animals, and men were not in such a fleshly body as they have today; men had no bony system. All that was formed later. The farther we look back, the nearer we come to a condition which, if we could have observed it from cosmic distances, we would have seen as a mist, as a fine etheric

13

cloud. This mist was much larger than our present earth, for it extended as far as the outermost planets of our solar system and even farther. It included a far-reaching nebular mass, wherein was contained all that went into the formation of the earth, and also of the planets and even of the sun.

If we could have examined this mass of mist closely, if an observer could have approached it, it would have seemed to be composed entirely of fine etheric points. When we see a swarm of gnats from a distance, it looks to us like a single cloud; close-up, however, we see the single insects. Thus, in the most remote past, the mass of our earth would have appeared, although then it was not material in our sense but was condensed only to an etheric condition. This earth-formation consisted of single ether-points, but something special was connected with these ether-points. Had the human eye been able to see these points, it would not have seen what the clairvoyant would have seen or what he actually sees now when he looks back. Let us make this clear by a comparison. Take the seed of a wild rose, a fully developed seed. What does one see who observes this? He sees a body that is very small, and if he did not know how a rose seed looked he would never imagine that a rose could grow from it. He would never derive this from the mere form of the seed. But a person who was endowed with a certain clairvoyant capacity would experience the following. The seed would gradually disappear from his sight, but to his clairvoyant eye would appear a flower-like form growing spiritually out of the seed. It would stand before his clairvoyant view, a real form, but one that could be seen only in the spirit. This form is the archetype of what later grows out of the seed. We would err if we believed that this form was exactly like the plant that grows from the seed. It is not at all like it. It is a wonderful light-form, containing streams and complicated formations. One could say that what later grows out of the seed is only a shadow of this wonderful spiritual light-form beheld by the clairvoyant.

Holding fast to this picture of how the clairvoyant sees the archetype of the plant, let us now return to the primeval earth and the single etheric points. If now, as in the previous example, the clairvoyant contemplated such an etheric point in the primeval substance, there would arise for him from the point (as from the seed in the previous example) a light-form, a beautiful form, which in reality is not there but rests slumbering in the point. What is this form that the seer perceives, looking back at the primal earth atom? What is it that arises? It is a form that is different from physical man, as different as is the archetype from the physical plant. It is the archetype of the present human form. At that time the human form slumbered spiritually in the etheric point, and the whole earth-evolution was necessary in order that what rested there might develop into present-day man. Many, many things were necessary for this, just as much is also necessary for the seed. This seed must be sunk in the earth, and the sun must send its warming rays, before it can develop itself into a plant. We will gradually understand how these points became men if we make clear to ourselves all that has happened in the meanwhile.

In the primeval past all the planets were connected with our earth. However, we will first consider the sun, moon, and earth because they are of special interest to us. At that time our sun, our moon, and our earth were not separate, but were all together. If we could stir these three bodies together like a broth in a great world-kettle, and if we thought of this as one cosmic body, we would have what the earth in its original condition was—sun plus earth plus moon. Naturally, man could live there only in a spiritual condition. He could live only in this condition because what is in the present sun was then united with the earth. For a long, long time the cosmic body contained our earth, sun, and moon within itself, as well as all the beings and forces connected with them. In those times man was still only present spiritually in the primal human atom. This changed only in a time when something important occurred in world-evolution, when the sun split off and became a separate body, leaving earth and moon behind.

After this, what was formerly a unity appears as a duality, as two cosmic bodies, the sun and the earth-plus-moon. Why did this occur?

All that happens has, naturally, a deep meaning, and we understand this when, looking backward, we find that there dwelt on earth at that time not only men but also other beings of a spiritual nature who were connected with them. These were not perceptible to the physical eye but were nevertheless present, as truly present as men and the other physical beings. Thus, for example, there are connected with our earth, living in its environs, beings whom Christian esotericism calls angels, Angeloi. We can best conceive these beings if we reflect that they stand at the stage at which man will be when the earth completes its evolution. Today these beings are already as far along as man will be at the end of his evolution on earth. A still higher stage is occupied by the archangels, Archangeloi, or Spirits of Fire, beings whom we can perceive when we direct our glance to what concerns entire peoples. Such concerns are guided by the beings called archangels or Archangeloi. A still higher type of being is called the Primal Beginnings or Archai or Spirits of Personality. We find these when we look at whole epochs of time and at many peoples, with all their connections and contrasts, contemplating what is usually called the Zeitgeist or Spirit of the Time. When we examine our own time, for example, we find that it is guided by higher beings called Archai or Primal Beginnings. Then there are still higher beings called, in Christian esotericism, Powers or Exusiai or Spirits of Form. Thus there are innumerable beings connected with our earth who are related to man in a sort of ladder of successive stages.

If we begin with the mineral and rise from the mineral to the plant, from the plant to the animal, and then to man, man is the highest physical being, but the others are also there; they are among us and permeate us. In the beginning of things, when the earth emerged from the womb of eternity as a sort of primeval mist, all these beings were bound up with the earth, and the clairvoyant would have seen how other beings pervade this picture at the same time as the human form. These were the beings named above, and beings of still higher types such as the Virtues, Dominions, Thrones, Cherubim, and finally the Seraphim. All of these beings were intimately connected with that powerful etheric dust, but they are at various stages of development. There are those whose sublimity man cannot fathom, but others are closer to him.

Since these beings were at different stages, they could not go through their evolution in the same way as man. A dwelling place had to be created for them. Among these high beings there were some who would have been greatly handicapped had they remained bound to lower beings. Therefore they split off. They took the finest substances out of the mist and built their dwelling in the sun. They created their heaven there, and there they found the proper tempo for their evolution. Had they remained in the inferior substances that they left behind in the earth, they would not have been able to continue their evolution. This would have hindered their development like a lead weight. This shows how material occurrences, such as the split in the cosmic substance, do not proceed from merely physical causes but rather from the forces of beings who need a site for their development. It happens because they must build their cosmic house. We must emphasize that spiritual causes lie at the foundation.

Man remained behind on the earth-plus-moon, and with him higher beings of the lowest hierarchy, such as angels and archangels, as well as beings who stood lower than man. But a single mighty being, who was already ripe enough to migrate to the sun, sacrificed himself and stayed with earth-plus-moon. This was the being who was later named Yahveh or Jehovah. He left the sun and became the leader of affairs on earth-plus-moon. Thus we have two dwelling-places: the sun and earth-plus-moon. On the sun were the most exalted beings, under the leadership of an especially high and sublime being whom the Gnostics attempted to conceive under the name Pleroma. We must picture this being as the regent of the sun. Yahveh is the leader of earth-plus-moon. We must make it especially clear that the noblest loftiest spirits

17

went out with the sun, leaving the earth behind with the moon. The moon was not yet split off; it was still within the earth.

How should one conceive this cosmic event of the separation of the sun from the earth? Above all, one must feel the sun and its inhabitants to be the most august, pure, and sublime element that was formerly connected with the earth, whereas earth-plus-moon was the lower element. At that time its condition was still lower than that of our present earth. The latter stands higher because there came a later period during which the earth unburdened itself of the moon and its grosser substances, in the presence of which man could not have developed further. The earth had to expel the moon.

Just before this, however, was the darkest and most dreadful time for our earth. Everything with a noble evolutionary disposition came under the control of bad forces, so that man could progress further only by eliminating the worst conditions of existence along with the moon.

We must realize that a sublime light-principle, that of the sun, was opposed to the principle of darkness, that of the moon. Had one clairvoyantly observed the sun, which had already withdrawn, one would have seen the beings who wished to inhabit it, but also something else would have been perceived. What had withdrawn itself as the sun would have shown itself not only as a cluster of spiritual beings, nor would it have appeared as something etheric, for that belongs to a coarser realm; it would have appeared as something astral, as a mighty light-aura. What one would have sensed as a light-principle, one would have seen as a shining aura in cosmic space. The earth, through allowing this light to go forth, would suddenly have appeared densified, though not yet coming to a firm mineral consistency. A good and an evil, a bright and a dark principle, stood opposed to each other at that time.

Now let us see how the earth looked before it expelled the moon. It would be entirely wrong to think of it as resembling our present earth. The core of the earth was then a fiery seething mass. This core would have appeared as a nucleus of fire surrounded by powerful water-forces, although these would not have been like our water of today, for they contained the metals in fluid form. In the middle of all this was man, but in entirely different form.

Thus the earth appeared when it expelled the moon. Air was not to be found on the earth; it simply was not there. The beings then existing needed no air; they had an entirely different breathing system. Man had become a sort of fish-amphibian, but he consisted of soft fluid material. What he sucked into himself was not air but what was contained in the water. This is approximately the way the earth looked at that time. We must see that the earth at that time was in a lower condition than at present. It had to be so. Otherwise man could never have been able to find the right tempo and the means for his evolution, if the sun and moon had not separated themselves from the earth. Had the sun remained in the earth, everything would have gone too fast; whereas everything would have gone too slowly with the forces that now work on the moon. As the moon withdrew from the earth amid tremendous catastrophes, there prepared itself slowly what we may call the separation of an air-sheath from the water-element. Air was then entirely different from the air of today, for all kinds of vapors were still contained in it. But the being that was then graddually preparing itself was a sort of sketch of the man of today. We will describe all this more fully later.

We have learned to know man in three relationships. First, as he lived in earth-plus-sun-plus-moon with all the higher beings in a single cosmic body. Here he presented himself to the clairvoyant eye in the way described above. Next we see him under unfavorable conditions on earth-plus-moon. Had he remained in this condition, he would have become a malicious and savage being. When the sun had separated itself, there was the contrast of the sun on one side and moon-plus-earth on the other side. The sun, in all its streaming glory, glittered as a great sun-aura in space. On the other side remained earth-plus-moon with all the sinister forces that drag down the nobler elements in man. A twofoldness arises, which is followed by a threefoldness. The sun remains as it is, but the earth separates itself from the moon. The grosser substances withdraw and man remains behind upon the earth.

Looking at the third period, man feels the forces as a threefold principle. He asks: Whence come these forces? In the first period man was still connected with all the high forces of the sun. The forces that developed in the second period then went out with the moon. Man felt this as a redemption, but he had a memory of the first period in which he was still united with the sun-beings. He learned to know what longing was; he felt himself to be a cast-off son. With the forces that had gone out with sun and moon he could feel himself as a son of the sun and of the moon.

So, our earth evolved from a unity to a duality to a trinity: sun, earth, and moon.

The time when the moon split away, when man first received the possibility of developing himself, is designated as the Lemurian epoch. After great fire-catastrophes had terminated this Lemurian epoch, our earth gradually entered a condition that could produce the relationships prevailing in ancient Atlantis. The first beginnings of land emerged from the water-masses. This was long after the moon broke away, yet it was only because of that breaking-away that the earth was able to evolve as it did.

In Atlantis man was entirely different from today, but he had reached the point where he could move about within the air-sheath as a soft, swimming, floating mass. Only gradually did he develop a bony system. About the middle of Atlantis he had progressed so far as somewhat to resemble our present form.

But in Atlantis man had a clairvoyant consciousness. Our present consciousness developed only in much later times, and if we wish to understand the man of that time we must bear this clairvoyant consciousness in mind. We can understand this best through a comparison with the consciousness of today. Today man perceives the world from morning to evening by means of his senses. Through his sense-activity he continually receives impressions of sight, hearing, etc. But at night this sense-world sinks into an ocean of unconsciousness. For the occultist, this is really

20

not so much a lack of consciousness as a lower grade of consciousness.

At this point we must make it clear that today man has a double consciousness, a bright day-consciousness and a sleep or dream consciousness. This was not at all the case in the first Atlantean times. Let us examine the alternation between waking and sleeping in those early times. During a certain period man dipped down into his physical body, but he did not perceive objects in the same sharp outlines as today. If we picture ourselves walking through a dense fog when the street lamps seem surrounded by a light-aura, we will have a rough idea of the Atlantean's object-consciousness. For the man of that time, everything was surrounded by such a fog; everything was as though enveloped in mist. That was the look of things by day. By night things looked entirely different, although still not the same as today. When the Atlantean went out of his body, he did not sink into unconsciousness but found himself in a world of divine spiritual beings, ego-beings, whom he perceived around him as his companions. As truly as man today does not see these beings at night, so truly did he in those times plunge into an ocean of spirituality, in which he actually perceived the divine beings. By day he was the companon of the lower kingdoms; by night he was the companion of the higher beings. Man lived in a spiritual consciousness, though this was dim; and though he had no self-consciousness, he dwelt among these divine spiritual beings.

Now let us recapitulate the four epochs in the evolution of our earth. First, let us bring to mind the epoch in which sun and moon were still united with the earth. We must say that the beings of this earth are pure ideal beings, while man is present only as an etheric body, visible only to spiritual eyes. Then we come to the second epoch. We see the sun as a separate body, visible as an aura, and moon-plus-earth as a world of evil. Then we come to a third epoch, where the moon separates itself and on earth there work the forces that are the result of this threeness. Then we come to a fourth epoch. Here man is already a being in the physical world, which seems misty to him, and in sleep he is still the companion of divine beings. This is the epoch that closes with huge water-catastrophes, the time of Atlantis.

Now let us go one step further, to the man of the post-Atlantean time. As stated earlier, he has evolved through many thousands of years. We see him pass through the cultural epochs of the post-Atlantean time; the ancient Indian, the ancient Persian, the Egypto-Chaldean-Babylonian, the Greco-Latin culture, and our fifth culture. What, above all things, had man lost? He had lost something that we can conceive when we bear the description of Atlantis in mind.

Let us try to imagine the sleep-condition of the Atlantean. Man was then still the companion of the gods; he actually perceived a world of the spirit. This he had lost after the Atlantean catastrophe. The darkness of night surrounded him. In recompense there came a brightening of the day-consciousness and the development of the ego. All this man had achieved, but the old gods had vanished from his sight; they were now only memories. In fact, during the first post-Atlantean time all that his soul had experienced was merely a memory, a memory of his earlier intercourse with these divine beings.

We know that souls endure, that they reincarnate. Just as in ancient Atlantean times our souls were already present, were already living in bodies, so were they also present at the separation of moon and sun from the earth, and also in the earliest times of all. Man existed in the etheric dust or points, and the five cultural periods of the post-Atlantean time, in their views of the world, in their religions, are nothing else than memories of the ancient epochs of the earth.

The first period, the primeval Indian, developed a religion that seems like an inner lighting-up, an inner repetition, in ideas and feelings, of the very first period, when sun and moon were still bound up with the earth, when the lofty beings of the sun still dwelt on earth. We may imagine that this had to awaken a sublime view. The spirit who, in the first condition of the earth, in the primeval mist, connected himself with all angels, archangels, high gods, and spiritual beings, was for Indian consciousness summed up as a single high individuality under the name of Brahm or Brahma.* This first post-Atlantean culture recapitulated in the spirit what had happened earlier. It is a repetition of the first epoch of the earth, in its inner aspect.

Now let us look at the second cultural period. In the principles of light and darkness we have the religious consciousness of the primeval Persian period. The great initiate saw an opposition between two beings, one of which was personified in the sun and the other in the moon. Ahura Mazdao or Ormuzd, the Light-aura, is the being whom the Persians venerated as the highest god. Ahriman is the evil spirit, the representative of all the beings who belonged to earth-plus-moon. The religion of the Persians is a remembrance of the second epoch of the earth.

In the third cultural epoch, man had to say to himself, "In me are the forces of the sun and of the moon; I am a son of the sun and a son of the moon. All the forces of the sun and of the moon appear as my father and my mother." Thus we have *unity* in the primeval past as the attitude of the Indian; while the *duality* that appeared with the separation of the sun is reflected in the religion of the Persians; and in the religious views of the Egyptians, Chal-

* It may occur to the reader that India, even in ancient times, was notable for the multiplicity of its gods rather than for their unity. In this connection the following passage from the Upanishads may be illuminating:

Then Vidagda Sakayla questioned him: "How many gods are there, Yajnavalkya?"

He answered: "As many as are mentioned in the Hymn to All the Gods, namely three hundred and three, and three thousand and three."

"Yes, but just how many gods are there, Yajnavalkya?"
"Thirty-three."
"Yes, but just how many gods are there, Yajnavalkya?"
"Six."
"Yes, but just how many gods are there, Yajnavalkya?"
"Two."
"Yes, but just how many gods are there, Yajnavalkya?"
"One and a half."
"Yes, but just how many gods are there, Yajnavalkya?"
"One."

(Brih. Upan., ii, 2, iv, 4.)

23

deans, Assyrians, and Babylonians we find the *trinity* that appeared in the third epoch, after the separation of sun and moon. Trinity appears in all the religions of the third period, and in Egypt it is exemplified in Osiris, Isis, and Horus.

But what man had experienced in his consciousness in the fourth earth-epoch, the Atlantean, as a companion of the gods, emerges as a memory in the Greco-Latin period. The gods of the Greeks are nothing other than memories of the gods whose companion man was in Atlantis, the gods whom he saw clairvoyantly in etheric forms when he had risen out of his physical body at night. As truly as man today sees outer objects, so truly at that time did he see Zeus, Athena, etc. For him these were real figures. What the Atlantean felt and experienced in his clairvoyant condition reappeared, for the man of the fourth post-Atlantean period, in the pantheon. As the Egyptian time was a memory of the trinity that prevailed in the Lemurian epoch, the experience of Atlantis remained as a memory in the Hellenic hierarchy of gods. In Greece and elsewhere in Europe these were the same gods whom the Atlantean had seen, but under other names. These names were not invented; they are names for the same forms that walked beside man in the Atlantean time when he went out of his physical body.

So we see how the epochs of cosmic events find their symbolical expression in the religious views of the different post-Atlantean cultural periods. What took place during sleep in the Atlantean time lives again in the fourth period.

We are in the fifth post-Atlantean period. What can we remember? In the first period the ancient Indians could conceive the first earth-epoch; in the second period the Persians had the principles of good and evil; the ancient Egyptians could picture the third epoch in its trinity. The period of the Greeks, the old Germans, the Romans, had its Olympus. It remembered the godlike figures of Atlantis. Then came the modern time, the fifth period. What can it remember?

It can remember nothing. This is the reason why in this period godlessness has been able to make headway in many respects.

This is why the fifth period is driven to look toward the future rather than the past. It must look toward the future, when all the gods must arise again. This reunion with the gods was prepared in the time of the bursting-in of the Christ-force, which worked so powerfully that it could again endow man with a godly consciousness. The god-pictures of the fifth period cannot be memories. Only if man looks forward will life again become spiritual. In the fifth post-Atlantean period, consciousness must become *apocalyptic*.

Yesterday we examined the relations of the single cultures of the Post-Atlantean time. Today we have seen how cosmic events are reflected in the religious views of these cultures.

Our fifth period stands at a central point in the world, hence it must look forward. The Christ must for the first time be fully grasped in this period, for our souls are deeply interwoven in mysterious connections. We shall see how the repetition of the Egyptian time in our fifth period gives us a point of departure, and how we can actually pass over into the future.

LECTURE 3

The Old Initiation Centers.
The Human Form as the Subject
of Meditation.

September 4, 1908

YESTERDAY we spoke of the mysterious connection between the earlier evolutionary conditions of our earth and the various world-conceptions of the successive post-Atlantean periods. The remarkable fact emerged that when the Atlantean catastrophe had altered the face of the earth, the holy pre-Vedic Indian culture, in its philosophical conceptions, showed something like a mirror-picture of the events that, in the beginning of the earth's evolution, took place in that remote past when sun, moon, and earth were still united. What the eye of the spirit beheld at that time was nothing but a spiritually conceived form of what actually existed when our earth stood at the beginning of its evolution.

The second condition of the earth, when the sun had detached itself but earth and moon still formed one body, came to light during the second cultural period, the old Persian, as a philosophic-religious system in the opposition of the light-principle in the sun-aura to the principle of darkness, the opposition of Omuzd to Ahriman. The third period, the Egyptian-Babylonian-Assyrian, is a spiritual reflection of what took place when earth, sun, and moon had become three bodies. We also pointed out that the trinity of Osiris, Isis, and Horus reflected the third epoch's astral trinity of sun, earth, and moon.

This separation occurred in the Lemurian time. After this followed the Atlantean time, the fourth evolutionary condition of the earth, in which there prevailed conditions of consciousness entirely different from those of today. Through these different forms of consciousness man lived with the gods, he was acquainted with the gods who were later named Wotan, Balder, Thor, Zeus, Apollo, etc. These were beings whom the Atlantean man could perceive with his clairvoyance. We have a repetition of the Atlantean perception of divine-spiritual beings in the memory of the peoples of the Greco-Latin time, and also among the peoples of northern Europe. It was a memory of the experiences of earlier conditions of consciousness. Be it Wotan or Zeus, be it Mars, Hera, or Athena, all were a memory of the spirit-forms of that old world of gods.

Today we must gradually penetrate a little more into the souls of the ancient Indian, Persian, and Egyptian cultures. If we want to form a true picture of the religious experiences of these ancient cultures, we must bear in mind that the most important parts of the population among these ancient peoples, including the seers, prophets, and enlightened persons, were successors of men who had already lived in the Atlantean time. Furthermore, it was by no means the case that the whole of Atlantean culture was destroyed immediately after the great catastrophe; on the contrary, what remained was gradually carried over and planted into the new time. We will best understand the souls of the post-Atlantean descendants if we steep ourselves in the soul-life of the last Atlanteans.

In the latter Atlantean time men were different one from another, some having retained a high degree of clairvoyant ability. This faculty did not vanish suddenly, but was still present in

27

many of the men who took part in the great migration from west to east. In others, however, it had already disappeared. There were advanced persons and retarded persons and, in accordance with the whole nature of evolution at that time, we can understand that the least advanced were those who were the most clairvoyant, for in a certain way they had remained stationary and had preserved the old Atlantean character. The most advanced were those who had already achieved a physical perceiving of the world, thus approaching our form of day-consciousness. It was they who ceased to see the spiritual world clairvoyantly at night, and who during their waking hours saw objects with sharper contours. That little handful of whom we have already spoken, who were led by the greatest initiate (generally known as Manu*) and his pupils deep into Asia and thence fructified the other cultures, just this handful, being composed of the most advanced men of that time, first lost the ancient gift of clairvoyance for the ordinary relationships of life. For them the true day-consciousness, in which we see physical objects sharply contoured, became ever clearer. Their great leader led this group farthest into Asia, so that they could live in isolation; otherwise they would have come too closely in touch with other peoples who still preserved the old clairvoyance. Only because they remained separated from other peoples for a time could they grow into a new type of man. A colony was established in inner Asia, whence the great cultural streams could flow into the most varied peoples.

Northern India was the first country to receive its new cultural current from this center. It has already been pointed out that these little groups of cultural pioneers nowhere found unpopulated territory. Earlier still, before their great migration from west to east, there had been other wanderings, and whenever new stretches of land rose from the sea, they were peopled by the wanderers. The persons sent out from this colony in Asia had to mix with other peoples, all of whom were more backward than they who had been led by Manu. Among these other peo-

* Echoes of this term were preserved by many peoples: e.g. Menes in Egypt, Manu in India, Minos in Crete, and Manitu in America.

ples were many persons who had retained the old clairvoyance.

It was not the custom of the initiates to establish colonies as this is done today; they colonized in a different way. They knew that they had to start with the souls of the persons whom they met in the lands that were to be colonized. The emissaries did not impose what they had to say. They reckoned with what they found. A balance was reached that took into account the needs of the old inhabitants. This reckoned with their religious views, which were based on the memory of earlier epochs, and also with the old clairvoyant disposition. So it was natural that only a handful of the most advanced could develop true concepts. The great masses could form only ideas that were a sort of compromise between the old Atlantean and the post-Atlantean attitudes. Therefore, we find in all these countries, in India, in Persia, in Egypt, whenever the different post-Atlantean cultures appeared, religious ideas which for that age are less advanced, less cultivated; which are nothing but a sort of continuation of the old Atlantean ideas.

To understand what kind of conceptions really appeared in these folk-religions we must form a picture of them. We must transport ourselves into the souls of the last Atlantean population. We must bear in mind that in the Atlantean time man was not unconscious at night, but that he could then perceive just as he perceived by day—if we can speak at all of night or day in that time. By day he perceived the first traces of what we today so clearly see as the world of sense-perceptions. By night he was the companion of the divine spiritual beings. He needed no proof of the existence of gods, just as we today need no proof of the existence of minerals. The gods were his companions; he himself was a spiritual being during the night. In his astral body and ego he wandered about the spiritual world. He was himself a spirit and he met beings who were of like nature with himself.

Naturally, man did not meet only these higher spiritual beings. He also met beings lower than those who were later known as Wotan, Zeus, etc. These were the choicest figures, but by no means the only ones. It was like seeing kings and emperors today. Many do not see them, yet still believe that there are kings and emperors.

In this state, which was common to everyone, man perceived the surrounding objects in a way different from his perception today. This was true even while he was conscious during the day. We must try to understand what this consciousness of the latter Atlanteans was.

We have described how the divine beings became imperceptible to man when he dived down into his physical body in the morning. He saw objects as though they were surrounded by mist. These were the images of his waking day at that time. But these pictures had another remarkable property, which we must grasp clearly. Let us suppose that such a man approached a pond. He did not see the water in the pond so clearly defined as we do today, but when he directed his attention to it he experienced something quite different. In approaching the pond a feeling arose in him, merely through looking at it, that was like a taste of what lay before him physically, without his having to drink the water. Simply through looking at it he would have felt that the water was sweet or salty. It was not at all like our seeing water today. We see only the surface and do not penetrate into the inner qualities. But while a dim clairvoyance still prevailed, the man who approached the pond had no alien feeling toward it. He felt himself as being within the properties of the water; he did not stand over against the object as we do; it was as though he could penetrate into the water.

If we had encountered a block of salt at that time, we would have noticed its taste as we approached it. Today we must lick it before we perceive what was then given through mere sight. Man was, as it were, within the whole, and he perceived things as though they were ensouled. He perceived beings that imparted a salty taste to the block. Everything was ensouled for him; air, earth, water, fire. Everything revealed something to him. He could feel himself into the interior of objects; he experienced their inner essence. Nothing appeared to him as a soulless object in the modern way. Therefore man felt everything with sympathy and antipathy because he saw its inner nature. He felt, he experienced, the inner being of the objects.

Memories of these experiences remained everywhere. The parts of the Indian population encountered by the colonists had such a relation to things. They knew that souls lived in things. They had preserved the ability to see the properties of things. Let us bear in mind this whole relationship of men to things. At that time man could perceive how the water tasted as he approached the pond. There he saw a spiritual being, who gave the water its taste. He could meet this spiritual being during the night if he lay down by the water and fell asleep. By day he saw the material; by night he saw what lived in things. By day he saw stones, plants, and animals, he heard the wind blow and the waters roar; by night he saw within himself, in its true form, what he only sensed by day—the spirits that live in all things. When he said that spirits live in the minerals, in the plants, in the water, in the clouds, in the wind, this was for him no poetic license, no mere fantasy, but something that he could see.

We must live deeply into these souls in order to understand them. Then we understand what dreadful folly it is when our scholars speak of animism and allege that it is the "folk-imagination" that ensouls and personifies things. There is no such folk-imagination. One who really knows the folk does not speak in this way. Repeatedly we find this singular analogy; just as a child, bumping against a table, strikes the table in revenge because (so say the scholars) it thinks of the table as having a soul, so did the primeval man in his childishness ensoul the objects of nature, such as the trees. This is repeated *ad nauseam*. Certainly there is imagination here, but it is the imagination of the scholars rather than of the folk. It is the scholars who are dreaming. Those who originally saw everything as ensouled were not dreaming; they only reported what they actually saw.

As a sort of remnant, this kind of perception emerged among the ancient peoples as a memory. But the error in the above analogy is that the child does not see the table as ensouled; he does not yet feel a soul in himself, but regards himself as a lump

31

of wood. Feeling himself soulless, he places himself on the same level as the soulless table that he bangs. The fact is just the opposite of what we read in the learned books. Whether we look at India, Persia, Egypt, Greece, or any other place, we find everywhere the same images that were described above, and into these images was poured the culture that was given out by the old initiates.

In ancient India the Rishis guided the culture. We must try to understand something of what gave the impulse to a form that developed into one of the most important forms of the Indian outlook. We know that in all ages there have been so-called mystery schools, where those who could develop their spiritual faculties learned to see more deeply into the world-all, awakening the slumbering faculties so as to see the spiritual connections of things. From these mystery-places proceeded the spiritual impulses of the various cultures. In order really to understand the initiates, we usually consider them as they were in post-Atlantean times, since their nature at that time is most easily comprehensible. But in Atlantis we could encounter something similar to initiate-schools. In order to understand them thoroughly, let us examine the methods of such an ancient Atlantean initiation-school.

If we go back to those times, we find that the above-described conditions of consciousness prevailed and also that man did not then have his present shape. He had quite a different form.* Let us go back to the first half of the Atlantean period. Man consisted already of physical, etheric, and astral bodies, plus the ego, but the physical body still looked quite different. We might compare it with the bodies of certain sea-animals, transparent, hardly to be seen, although laced with luminous threads in certain directions. It was much softer than today, having as yet no bones. It is true that there was already cartilage in some parts, but in these

---

* The genesis of the human form is much discussed in this and succeeding chapters. The reader will find Dr. H. Poppelbaum's book *Man and Animal* (Rudolf Steiner Press, London, 1960) to be a helpful companion in this study.

ancient times the physical body was definitely not of its present form.

The etheric body was a much more important member. The physical body was then more or less the same size as now, but the etheric body was extraordinarily large. This etheric body varied among individuals, but one could perceive four different types. One part of mankind would resemble one type, another part another. These four types may be designated by the names of the apocalyptic beasts: bull, lion, eagle, man. It would not be correct to imagine that these beasts were exactly similar to the present animals, but the impression that they made reminds us of these. The impressions that the etheric bodies made can be understood through the picture of a lion, bull, eagle, or man. We can compare with the bull the portion of mankind that gave the impression of having powerful reproductive forces or an unusual appetite. Another portion lived more in the spiritual; these were the eagle men, who felt less at home in the physical world. Then there were men in whom the etheric body was already similar to the present-day physical body; it was not quite identical, but it was like the human form. However, we must not imagine that each man represented only one type; all four types would show some traces in each person, but one or another would predominate.

Such were the etheric bodies of the Atlantean population. As to the astral body, it was especially powerful but largely undeveloped, while the ego was still wholly outside of man. People were entirely different at that time from today. Naturally, some men matured earlier and assumed the ultimate form before the others, but in the main one can describe the men of that time as we have just done. This was the normal condition of the average man.

It was entirely different with the more advanced persons, with the pupils of the mystery-places, who strove after the initiation of the ancient Atlantis. Let us enter in spirit such a center of initiation and try to picture what the teacher had to give. First, what was this teacher himself?

33

If one meets an initiate today, there is nothing in his general appearance by which he can be recognized. Few persons would recognize him today. The initiate must live in a physical body, and the physical body has developed a long way; hence it differs from others only in certain inner refinements. At that time, however, the initiate was vastly different from other men. The others still had a more animal-like form; the physical body was small in comparison with the gigantic etheric bodies, forming a clumsy animal-like mass. The initiate differed from these in that his physical body was more similar to the modern formation; his countenance was similar to that of modern man, and he had a forebrain such as that of the average man of today. His brain was highly developed, which was not true of other men at that time. These initiates had their schools, into which they admitted pupils who, having proved themselves mature and sufficiently developed, were selected out of the ordinary run of men by special methods.

We must bear one thing in mind if we wish fully to understand what follows. We must realize that in the course of time the power of man's spiritual members over his physical body has almost completely disappeared. The man of today has a certain degree of control over his body. He can move his arms and legs, pedal on bicycles, and exercise some command over his physiognomy, but this is only a last meager remnant of the mastery over the physical body that obtained in ancient Atlantean times. In those days the thoughts and feelings had a much greater influence over the physical body. If today a person were to concentrate for weeks, months, or even years on a certain thought, only in exceptional cases would this influence more than the etheric body. Seldom would the physical body be influenced by a meditation. If, for example, someone should succeed by this means in making his brain move further forward, thus working even on the bones of his forehead, this would be an astounding achievement. Very, very seldom does this happen today. Extraordinary energy would have to be developed today for a thought to work on the physical body. It is easier to affect the blood-circulation or the breathing, but even this is difficult. Thoughts can work on the etheric body today, and in the next incarnation they will have worked so powerfully as to alter the external physical structure. Man should work today in the knowledge that he is working not for *one* incarnation but for many incarnations to come. The soul is eternal; it continually returns.

Things were different in the ancient initiation schools. Thinking had such mastery there that it could influence the physical body in a comparatively short time. The pupil of the mysteries could mold his own organization until it resembled the human. One could accept a pupil out of the normal run of men and had only to give him the right impulse. The pupil himself did not have to think; through a sort of suggestion thoughts were implanted in his soul. A definite spiritual form had to stand before his soul, and the pupil had to steep himself in this form. Everywhere the Atlantean initiates gave to their pupils a thought-form, into which the pupils had to immerse themselves over and over again. What kind of picture was this? What did the pupil have to think? What did he meditate on?

We have already pointed to the original condition of the earth, sketching out the whole of evolution and mentioning the light-form in the primeval dust. Had one at that time looked about clairvoyantly, the archetype of the man of today would have arisen. This grew out of that pollen, out of that primeval atom. Not the form of ancient man or of Atlantean man, but the form of modern man grew out of that atom. And what did the Atlantean initiate do? He placed before the soul of his pupil precisely this archetype that reared itself out of the primeval seed.

The pupil had to meditate on this archetype. The initiate placed before the pupil's gaze the human shape as a thought-form, with all the impulses and feelings that were contained in it. Whether the pupil was of the lion type or of one of the others, he had to hold before himself this picture of what man was to become in post-Atlantean times. He received this thought-picture as an ideal. He had to will the thought, "My physical body must become like this picture." Through the power of this picture his body was so influenced that it became different from the bodies of other men. Certain parts were transformed, and gradually the most advanced pupils became more similar to the man of today.

Thus we look back on remarkable mysteries, the mysteries of ancient Atlantis. No matter how the various men might be formed, there floated before their souls, as a picture, a thing that was already present as a spiritual picture when the sun was still united with the earth. This picture emerged more and more as the meaning of the earth, as what lies spiritually at the foundation of the earth. This picture did not appear to them as this or that form, as the picture of this or that race; it appeared to them as the universal ideal of mankind.

This is the feeling that the pupil was to develop through this picture: "The highest spiritual beings have willed this picture, through which unity comes into mankind. This picture is the meaning of the earth's evolution; to bring this picture to realization the sun separated itself from the earth and the moon detached itself. Through this man could become man. This is the One who will at last appear as the high ideal of the earth."

Into this high ideal streamed the feelings that enlivened the pupil in his meditation.

So did things stand about the middle of the Atlantean epoch. We will see later how this picture, which stood before the pupil as the human form, transformed itself into something different, and how this was salvaged after the Atlantean catastrophe. This is what lived again in the Indian initiation-teaching, where it was summed up in the ancient sacred name of Brahm. What the Godhead willed as the meaning of the earth was the most sacred thing for the ancient Indian initiate. He spoke of it as Brahma. From this sprang later Zarathustra's teaching and the Egyptian wisdom, both of which will be discussed later. How it transformed itself from Brahma to the Egyptian wisdom we will see tomorrow.

LECTURE 4

The Experiences of Initiation.
The Mysteries of the Planets.
The Descent of the Primeval Word.

September 5, 1908

YESTERDAY we closed with the discussion of an extraordinarily important event in the inner life, in the real spiritual life of man. We attempted to bring before our souls an impression that the seeker for initiation had at the beginning of the last third of the Atlantean epoch. We saw how there stood before the soul of the neophyte an ideal human form, a thought-picture, on which he had to concentrate in meditation, and how this filled the would-be initiate's life of thinking, feeling and willing. This thought-picture had to become ever more the model for the man of the future.

Now we must try to conceive roughly how this thought-picture looked. It was not entirely similar to the man of today. If we can think of a kind of combination of man and woman in which the lower part is omitted, a sort of double figure in which only the upper part of the body is clearly perceptible, then we have the sensible-supersensible picture that stood before the meditating person at that time. This picture worked so strongly that the neophytes could make their external bodies actually resemble it.

It is important that the meditating neophyte had within him, facing him, a sort of human form. If he had been sufficiently prepared to have this picture livingly before him, then he had to realize the following clearly, "As I look upon this picture I transport myself into the earliest condition of the earth's evolution, when earth, moon, and sun were not yet divided. At that time the earth consisted of the primeval atom, but in this atom the clairvoyant could see the picture that now arises before me. This picture was already present at the beginning of the earth when as yet there were no mineral, plant, or animal forms. At that time the earth consisted only of the human atom, of reawakened human beings."

It is true that the first beginnings of the animals were created during the ancient Moon condition of the earth; animals already existed then.* But we know too that a planetary system, when it disappears, goes into a pralaya, in which all forms are dissolved. Thus, although the ancient Moon was already populated with animal forms, the earth at first contained nothing similar to animals and plants. These first appeared later. Only after the separation of the sun did the animals gradually appear. The earth was purely human in its first beginnings.

The neophyte looked back upon this primeval condition of the earth. He saw in the primeval atom the ideal human form. Keeping this form before him, he realized, "Thus I transport myself into the earliest condition of the earth. What lives in the earth, the ideal human picture or form, tells me that the Godhead works from eternity to eternity. It has poured itself out into these forms. It has breathed out this original human form." Then he asked himself what happened to the animals, plants, and other beings.

* Throughout this and the following lectures much is said of the development of human and animal forms. For an attempt to systematize Dr. Steiner's views in this field and to bring them into connection with ordinary scientific knowledge, the reader is again referred to Poppelbaum, *Man and Animal* (Rudolf Steiner Press, London, 1960).

In spirit the neophyte saw the primal form of the Godhead. He saw the animals and plants as accompanying forms, which appeared on earth only at a later time. Everything in the lower kingdoms was regarded by the Atlantean neophyte as having proceeded from the human form. We understand this thought if we recollect how coal is formed. Think of the huge primeval forests that once flourished and are now coal. The plants have remained behind, evolving out of a higher kingdom into a lower one. The plants have hardened into stone.

Thus the pupil of the Atlantean mysteries saw everything in the world about him as the product of the human form. In primeval times, this impression was conjured before the soul of man. These impressions were retained in memory through the time of the flood. The ancient Indian initiators again called up in the souls of their pupils this picture of primeval man, of the man who had been breathed forth by the eternal self. When the Indian pupil had this picture before him, he felt that everything had sprung from it, that what appeared in this picture as the blood had become the waters of the earth, etc. This picture expanded until it became the foundation of the universe. Then the following was put before his soul. It was said to him, "In this picture you have two things before your eyes. First, the picture itself; but then, also, what lights up in you as your innermost essence when you contemplate this picture. Without is the macrocosm; within you is what you feel as a sort of extract, the microcosm."

When the Greeks, under Alexander, pressed into India and met the last echoes of what the pupils had felt in ancient times, they experienced the following: When the pupil contemplates what is spread out in the universe as man, then he has Heracles before him. The Indians gave the name of *Vach** to what lives as the forces of the world-all. But in man, as a sort of extract of the whole, they felt what they called *Brahman*. Thus the

* The Sanscrit word is *Vach* or *Vac*; see Maurice Bloomfield's *Religion of India* (New York, Putnam, 1908), pages 191 and 243. Dr. Steiner uses WHA in German, but the first letter should be pronounced like the English V, hence the WHA becomes VHA in English.

Greeks expounded these echoes of what occurred in the soul of the pupil of the ancient holy Indian culture. This was the fruit of the Greek's campaign to India under Alexander the Great.

Out of precisely this fundamental feeling developed the sacred doctrine of the ancient Indian initiates, which appears like a spiritual image of that primeval state of the earth when it still contained the sun-forces and high beings, for whose sublimity man later yearned. Hence it was a great moment in his spiritual life when the pupil was initiated and could allow to arise within him what was grasped as Brahman. This was a mighty event in the human soul. It was a rising into higher worlds. In no other way could a man be initiated and achieve real vision, than by rising into higher worlds.

The world around us is the physical world. Within and around it surges the astral world. Higher stands Devachan, the world of the gods. The pupil must penetrate to the highest regions of Devachan if he is to feel Brahman, the primeval self, in the macrocosm. Then he is in highest Devachan, the world of the gods, whence springs the noblest that is in man. It was a realm of the highest and most perfect order into which the pupil was transported, a realm that offered much knowledge in addition to what has been described here.

Before we go any further, we must learn to know the teachers also. All of you have heard of the holy Rishis, who were the original founders of the ancient holy Indian culture and had Manu for their own teacher. Who were these seven great teachers of ancient India? As far as possible, we must explain the nature of the holy Rishis. This requires us to look again into the universe. We must be quite clear that what we perceive with the physical senses is a result of what is spiritual. If we think of the entire surrounding world as spiritualized, we can compare it with a primeval etheric mist. This mist then gradually became denser; it descended into the condition of matter and the various heavenly bodies condensed out of it. Sun, Moon, and Earth detached themselves.

But why did the other planets split off? For it also occurred that Saturn, Jupiter, Mars, Venus, and Mercury detached themselves. Why did this happen? We shall understand this if we realize that in the great universe there occurs something similar to an event in our trivial everyday life. It is not only in school that pupils sometimes fail to be promoted, but also in the cosmos there are beings who remain behind and cannot progress with the others. Let us be quite clear about this. There was one group of higher beings who could not continue with the earth's tempo. These abstracted the finest substances and formed therefrom the sun as their dwelling-place. These were the highest beings connected with our evolution, although they also had gone through an evolution of their own. Thus there were beings who were in the act of becoming sun-spirits, and others who had remained behind, standing lower than the sun-spirits but higher than man. These could not continue with the sun-spirits because they were not equally mature. They could not go out with the sun, for it would have scorched them. But on the other hand they were too noble for the earth. Therefore they abstracted certain substances, which were between sun and earth in fineness and corresponded to their nature, and built themselves dwelling-places between the sun and the earth. Thus Venus and Mercury were separated off. Here we have two groups of beings who are not as high as the sun-spirits, but are further along than man. They became the spirits of Venus and Mercury. These are the beings who caused the appearance of these two planets. Mars, Jupiter and Saturn were formed earlier for other reasons, and they also became dwelling-places for certain beings.

Thus we see how spirits caused the appearance of these planets. Now one should not believe that these beings inhabiting the various bodies of the solar system have no connection with the inhabitants of the earth. We must see that the physical boundaries are not the real boundaries, and that it is possible for the beings of the other heavenly bodies to exercise magical influences upon the earth. Thus the influences of the spirits of the Sun, Mars, Jupiter, Saturn, Venus, and Mercury extend into the earth. The two latter stand nearer to the earth, and after the sun

41

had withdrawn they helped men to prepare the earth as we have it today.

Here I would like to add one thing, because misunderstandings have crept into the naming of the planets. In all occult nomenclature, what the astronomers call Venus is called Mercury, and vice versa. Astronomers know nothing of the mysteries behind this, because in the past it was not desired that the esoteric names should be revealed. This happened in order to conceal certain things.

All these spirits of the other planets influence the earth. From every planet influences descend upon man. To begin with, however, these influences had need of an intermediary. Through the great Manu this was provided by the seven Rishis being initiated in such a way that each understood the mysteries and influences of a single planet. Since there were seven planets there were seven Rishis, who collectively formed a sevenfold lodge that could transmit to the pupils the secrets of the solar system. We find hints of this in many ancient occult writings. When, for example, it is said that there are mysteries beyond the seven, the reference is to those preserved by the holy Manu himself concerning the time before the splitting-off of the planets.

The forces preserved by the planets were the subject of the mysteries of the seven Rishis. This choir of seven Rishis, in complete harmony with Manu, cooperated in the wonderful wisdom that was transmitted to the pupils. If we were to characterize this, we would have to say that this primeval teaching contained approximately what we learn today as the evolution of humanity through the planetary conditions of Saturn, Sun, Moon, Earth, Jupiter, Venus, and Vulcan. The mysteries of evolution were secreted in the seven members of the lodge, each of whom typified one stage in the progress of humanity.

The pupil saw this—not only saw it, but heard it—when he raised himself into Devachan, into the Devachanic world, for this is a world of tones. There he heard the harmony of the spheres, of the seven planets. In the astral world he saw the *picture;* in the Devachanic world he heard the *tone;* and in the highest world he experienced the *word*. When the Indian pupil raised himself into upper Devachan he perceived through the music of the spheres and through the word of the spheres how the primordial spirit, Brahma, is divided through evolution into the sevenfold planetary chain. He heard this out of the primal word *Vach*. This was the designation of the primal tone of creation that the pupil heard. In it he heard the entire world-evolution. The word, split into seven members, the primal word of creation, worked in the soul of the pupil; this was the primal word, which he described to the uninitiated approximately as we today would describe our world evolution. What he perceived is described in an elementary way in my book, *Theosophy, An Introduction to Supersensible Knowledge*. The description we find again in the ancient sacred tradition of the Indians, in what was called the *Veda,** or the Word. This is the true meaning of the Vedas, and what was later written down is only a last memory of the ancient sacred doctrine of the Word. The Word itself was only passed from mouth to mouth, for an ancient tradition is impaired by being written down. Only in the Vedas can one feel something of what flowed into this culture at that time. When the pupil experienced this in his memory, he could say to himself, "What I experience in my soul as Brahman, what I have in my soul as primal Word, this was already present on ancient Saturn; on Saturn resounded the first breath of the Veda-word."

Evolution had now progressed through the Sun and Moon stages, as far as the Earth. The word had become continually denser, had taken on ever denser forms, and the picture of man in the primeval seed of the earth was already a condensation of the condition in which the primeval word existed on Saturn. What had happened here?

The divine Word, primeval man, had sheathed itself in ever new coverings, and we must see what sheaths the Word assumed in the evolution of the earth. The pupil knew that nothing in the

* Selections from the *Vedas* are given in *Sacred Books of the East* (Oxford University Press, 1879–1910) but there seems to be no complete translation or index in English.

43

universe repeats itself exactly, and that each planet has its mission. What on the ancient Sun he saw shape itself as *life,* what on the ancient Moon was injected into the foundation of all things as *wisdom,* was followed by the task or mission of the Earth, which is to develop *love.* This was not yet present on the ancient Moon. What was present on the latter planet in a much more spiritual (but also in a much colder) form, the primal image of man, clothed itself in a warm astral covering. On the Moon, what man was supposed to become was clothed in a warm astral sheath, and it is this part which on Earth enables the inner human life to develop love from the lowest to the highest form.

To the Indian pupil the human form, the primal image, became clearly perceptible in higher Devachan. In lower Devachan it then surrounded itself with an astral sheath, which contained the forces for developing love. Love, or Eros, was called *Kama.** Thus Kama acquires a meaning for earth-evolution. The divine Word, Brahman, clothed itself in Kama, and through Kama the primal Word resounded to the pupil. Kama was the garment of love, the garment of the primal Word *Vach,* which lies at the root of the Latin *vox.*

In his innermost being the pupil felt that the divine Word had taken on an astral garment of love, and he said to himself, "Man, who today consists of four members, physical body, etheric body, astral body, and ego, has his ego as his highest member. This ego descended into the garment of love and formed Kama-Manas for itself. Kama, in which Manas clothed itself, was the innermost essence of man. This was the ego. But we know also that this innermost essence will evolve three higher members. These transform the lower members, transform even the physical body. As Manas grows out of the astral sheath, as Buddhi on a higher stage corresponds to Prana, so will the physical body, when it has been entirely spiritualized, be Atma."

All this already existed germinally in the Vach, and a verse of the Veda recalls how the pupil brought the mystery of the innermost being to expression.

* *Kama* is a Sanscrit word meaning *desire,* the nature of the astral body.

We know that the physical body first appeared on Saturn, the etheric on the Sun, the astral on the Moon, and the ego on the Earth. The true and original human germ, the primal Vach, however, already contained the three following members in itself. Man may still expect three higher members as well, and then only will he be a true image of the Word of creation, the primal Word. It was pointed out to the pupil that only to the initiate could the true nature of the physical, etheric and astral bodies be made clear. Today man is himself only when he expresses his "I am," when he keeps in mind what is entirely his own. Only then is he fully Man. The other members are manifest, but in them he is still unconscious. In the fourth, however, the Vach becomes manifest.

"In the fourth, Man speaks." This was the verse of the Veda. When the word of the ego resounds, the fourth part of the Vach resounds. The verse of the Veda reads, "Four parts of the Vach are manifest; three are visible; three are now concealed; in the fourth speaks Man."

Here we have a wonderful description of what we have so often heard. This stood before the pupil's spiritual perception. His gaze was directed backward to the condition in which nothing was as yet separate, in which there was still a primeval earth, in which the full Vach spoke. This is expressed in another verse of the Veda. "Formerly I knew not what the *I am* is. Only when the first-born of the earth came upon me did the spirit become filled with light, and I had a share in the holy Vach." In this is reproduced the vision that the initiate had.

In all this we have a hint of the experiences of the ancient pupils of the Rishis, of the wonderful teachings that flowed into the Indian culture, were transmitted to the following epochs, and were transformed in accordance with the needs of other peoples. But all of these understood the primeval Word, Vach.

We shall understand many things better if we keep in mind one mystery in its full scope. We must imagine that at that time the teacher's influence on the pupil was entirely different from what it is today. Such an influence is now possible only when the pupil has already been brought to a certain stage of initiation. The forces exerted by the teacher on the pupil were much stronger at that time. Not only what the teacher could transmit by word or writing had an effect. In reality, all this worked only on the intellectual soul, but apart from this, mysterious magical forces worked from the teacher to the pupil, and it was essentially the teacher's forces that were able to fill with brightness and living force the pictures that the teacher called up before the pupil's soul. This singular influence was lost only in the fourth post-Atlantean period, in the Greco-Latin culture. These forces simply change. When one of the old Egyptians confronted a young person, it was quite different from a teacher confronting a pupil today. Entirely different forces worked from age to youth. This will be recognized by anyone who seeks to understand what was still described in ancient Greece. Socrates actually had telepathic powers, which he allowed to work on his pupils while he instructed them. Such things can no longer work in our time, but they are hinted at in Plato's writings. What was entirely justified then would be rejected as a misdemeanor today. Changes take place, and today no one has a right to copy such methods. Certain phenomena today may remind us of this, but they must be considered reprehensible.

In ancient times, forces proceeded from the teacher to the pupil. Even in ancient Egypt there were still a great many people who could absorb forces in this manner. If a person who was especially sensitive stood before someone who had learned to strengthen his thoughts, a strong thought worked in such a way that it appeared as a picture in the soul of the sensitive person. In ancient Egypt such a telepathic influence was eminently possible, and thought-transference was present to a high degree. If a strong will-nature confronted someone who had not been strengthened, this was often the case. In Egypt one was able to guide and direct in a high degree through thoughts, in a way we today cannot imagine at all. Today such forces would be woefully misused. In ancient Egypt, however, initiation rested principally upon forces of this kind. This was likewise true in ancient India and Persia.

46

These forces also reinforced the method which, if an exoteric expression is desired, might be called medical. By this we do not mean the official medical practice of today. The Egyptian physician and initiate would have laughed to scorn what modern man calls medicine. The Egyptian physician knew one thing—that the conditions that prevailed in ancient Atlantis, and that could still be perceived in initiation, could in a certain sense be reawakened. The consciousness in which man lived in Atlantis was a dim clairvoyant consciousness. At that time (said the Egyptian initiate) the spiritual beings could exert a much greater influence on man. Today, when he sleeps, man knows nothing of the higher worlds, but the Atlantean, in his shadowy clairvoyant consciousness, then lived with the gods. If modern man can raise himself to an ideal, this is better for him than all moral teachings; similarly, the Egyptian initiate worked on his pupil through pictures of higher spiritual events. This had no mere external effect; it worked deeply within, and in such a way that a definite result ensued.

Let us think of a sick person, who is sick because certain bodily functions do not proceed in a normal way. What is the cause of this? A person with occult training knows that when the physical body functions irregularly, the cause does not lie outside the latter. On the contrary, all illnesses that do not come from outside the physical body, originate in the fact that the etheric body is not in order. But the etheric body is ill because the astral body is out of order. If an Atlantean was threatened with a disorder in the distribution of fluids, this was quickly taken care of. In a sleeping condition he received from the spiritual worlds such force that through his sleep the disturbed functions were restored to order, and he was brought back to health. He rebuilt the healing forces through sleep.

The ancient Egyptian physicians did something similar. They reduced the patient's consciousness to a sort of hypnotic sleep, during which they could govern the soul-pictures that arose around the patient. They guided these pictures in such a way that they were able to work back on the physical body and make it healthy. This was the significance of the temple-sleep that was applied for internal ailments. The patient was given no medicine,

47

but was allowed to sleep in the temple. His consciousness was damped down, and he was allowed to look into the spiritual worlds. Then his astral experiences were guided in such a way that they had the power to pour health into the body. This is no superstition; it is a secret that was known to the initiates. They introduced the spiritual into the patient's experiences. In this medical art, which we find so closely connected with the principle of initiation, the Atlantean conditions were artificially recreated during the healing. Since man did not work against himself through his day-consciousness, those forces could be active that were necessary for healing. This is how the temple-sleep worked.

In the Egyptian culture there still reigned that principle which, in India, reigned among those wise Rishis who guided affairs, who transmitted the planetary forces, who were the pupils of Manu, the great teacher of that first sublime culture. In the first post-Atlantean culture it was the Rishis who brought the sublime teaching that led men into lofty spiritual worlds, even into the world of higher devachan. In the succeeding cultural periods, what was seen there was led down as far as the physical plane. Until the fourth post-Atlantean period there continued to descend into the physical plane that Being whom we learned to know as Brahman in the Indian period and whom we now designate as Christ. No longer does he transmit the spiritual; he himself became man in order to radiate over all men the mysterious power of the primal Word.

Thus the primal Word descended, in order that it might lead man upward again. Man must understand how that happened, if he is to make himself an instrument through which he can work into the future. We must learn to know what happened before our time, so that we ourselves can cooperate in an ever higher molding of what exists around us and for us.

We must create a spiritual world in the future. To do this, we must first understand the cosmos.

LECTURE 5

The Genesis of the Trinity
of Sun, Moon, and Earth.
Osiris and Typhon.

September 7, 1908

UP to this point in these lectures we have tried to construct a picture of the earth's evolution in connection with the evolution of man, because we had to demonstrate how the earth's past, how the facts of its evolution, were reflected in the knowledge displayed by the various cultural periods of the post-Atlantean time. The deepest experiences of the pupils of the Rishis were characterized, and it was shown how these inner experiences of the neophyte portrayed, in inward clairvoyantly-perceived pictures, the relationships and events that prevailed in the primeval earth, when sun and moon were still contained in it. We also saw what a high stage of initiation such a pupil had to reach in order to build for himself such a world-conception, which appears as a recapitulation of what occurred in the remotest past. We also saw what the Greeks thought when, in the campaigns of Alexander, they became acquainted with what was experienced by such an Indian neophyte, in whose soul arose the picture of the

49

divine-spiritual creative force that began to express itself in the primeval mist when sun and moon were still united with the earth. This picture, the Brahman of the Indians, which was later called I-Brahma (Aham Brahma) and which appeared to the Greeks as Heracles—this picture, we sought to bring before our souls as an inner recapitulation of the facts that actually occurred in the past.

It was also emphasized that the succeeding evolutionary periods of the earth were reflected in the Persian and Egyptian cultures. What occurred in the second epoch, when the sun withdrew from the earth, appeared in pictures to the Persian initiates. All that happened as the moon gradually withdrew became the world-conception and the initiation-principle of the Egyptians, Chaldeans, Babylonians, Assyrians.

Now, in order to look quite clearly into the soul of the ancient Egyptian, which is the most important thing for us—and considering the Persian initiation only as a sort of preparation—we must examine a little more narrowly just what happened to our earth during the periods when the sun and moon were separating from it. We shall sketch how the earth itself gradually evolved during these times. We shall disregard the great cosmic events and direct our attention to what happened on the earth itself.

If again we look back on our earth in its primeval condition, when it was still united with sun and moon, we do not find our animals or plants, and especially not our minerals. At first the earth was composed only of man, only of the human germs. Of course it is true that the animal and plant germs were laid down on the old Sun and the old Moon, and that they were already contained in the earliest condition of the Earth, but in a certain way they were still slumbering, so that one could not perceive that they would really be able to bring forth anything. It was only when the sun began to withdraw that the germs that later became animals first became capable of germinating. Not until the sun had completely withdrawn from the earth, leaving earth and moon alone, did the same thing happen to the germs that later became plants. The mineral germs formed themselves gradually, only when the moon had begun to withdraw. We must keep this clearly in mind.

Now, for once, let us look at the earth itself. When it still had sun and moon within itself, the earth was only a sort of etheric mist of vast extent, within which the human germs were active, while the germs of the other beings—animals, plants, and minerals—slumbered. Since only human germs were present, there were no eyes to behold these events externally, hence the description given here is visible only for the clairvoyant vision in retrospect. It is given on the hypothesis that it is what one would have seen had one been able at that time to observe from a point in universal space.

On ancient Saturn, too, a physical eye would have seen nothing. In that primeval condition, the earth was merely a vaporous mist that could be felt physically only as warmth. Out of this mass, this primeval etheric mist, there gradually took shape a shining ball of vapor, which could have been seen had a physical eye been present. Could one have penetrated this with a feeling-sense, it would have appeared as a heated space, somewhat like the interior of an oven. But soon this mist became luminous, and this ball of vapor that thus took shape contained all the germs of which we have just spoken. We must be quite clear that this mist was nothing like a fog or cloud-formation of today; rather did it contain in solution all the substances which at present are solid or liquid. All metals, all minerals, everything, were then present in the mist in transparent and translucent form. There was a translucent vapor, permeated by warmth and light. Think yourself into this. What had grown out of the etheric mist was a translucent gas. This grew brighter and brighter, and through the condensation of the gases the light grew ever stronger, so that ultimately this vapor-mist appeared like a great sun that shone out into world-space.

This was the period when the earth still contained the sun, when the earth was still irradiated by light and rayed its light into world-space. But this light made it possible, not only that man should live with the earth in that primeval condition, but that in the fullness of the light there should also live all those other high beings who, although not assuming a physical body, were connected with the evolution of man: Angels, Archangels, and Principalities. But not only were these present. In the fullness of the light lived still higher beings also: the Powers, or Exusiai, or Spirits of Form; the Virtues, or Dynameis, or Spirits of Motion; the Dominions, or Kyriotetes, or Spirits of Wisdom; those spirits who are called the Thrones, or Spirits of Will; finally, in looser connection with the fullness of the light, more and more detaching themselves therefrom, the Cherubim and Seraphim. The earth was a world inhabited by a whole hierarchy of lower and higher beings, all sublime. What radiated out into space as light, the light with which the earth-body was permeated, was not light only but also what was later the mission of the earth: It was the force of love. This contained the light as its most important component. We must imagine that not only light was rayed forth, not physical light alone, but that this light was ensouled, inspirited, by the force of love. This is difficult for the modern mind to grasp. There are people today who describe the sun as though it were a gaseous ball that simply radiates light. Such a purely material conception of the sun prevails exclusively today. The occultists are the only exception. One who reads a description of the sun today as it is represented in popular books, in the books that are the spiritual nourishment of countless people, does not learn to know the true being of the sun. What these books say about the sun is worth about as much as if one described a corpse as the true being of man. The corpse is no more man than what astrophysics says of the sun is really the sun.

Just as one who describes a corpse leaves out the most important thing about man, so the physicist who describes the sun today leaves out the most important thing. He does not reach its essence, although he may believe that with the help of spectroanalysis he has found its inner elements. What is described is only the outer body of the sun.* In every sunbeam there streams down

* This sentiment as to the sun is eloquently expressed in English by D. H. Lawrence in his *Apocalypse* (New York, Viking, 1932), pp. 41–46.

on all the inhabitants of the earth the force of those higher beings who live on the sun, and in the light of the sun there descends the force of love, which here on earth streams from man to man, from heart to heart. The sun can never send mere physical light to earth; the warmest, most ardent, feeling of love is invisibly present in the sunlight. With the sunlight there stream to earth the forces of the Thrones, the Cherubim, the Seraphim, and the whole hierarchy of higher beings who inhabit the sun and have no need of any body other than the light. But since all this that is present in the sun today was at that time still united with the earth, those higher beings themselves were also united with the earth. Even today they are connected with earth-evolution.

We must reflect that man, the lowest of the higher beings, was at that time already present in the germ as the new child of the earth, borne and nourished in the womb by these divine beings. The man who lived in the period of earth-evolution that we are now considering, had to have a much more refined body, since he was still in the womb of these beings. The clairvoyant consciousness perceives that the body of the man of that time consisted only of a fine mist-form or vapor-form; it was a body of air or gas, a gas-body rayed through and entirely permeated by light. If we imagine a cloud formed with some regularity, a chalice-like formation expanding in an upward direction, the chalice glowing with inner light, we have the men of that time who, for the first time in this earth-evolution, began to have a dim consciousness, such a consciousness as the plant-world has today. These men were not like plants in the modern sense. They were cloud-masses in chalice-like form, illuminated and warmed by the light, with no firm boundaries dividing them from the collective earth-mass.

This was once the form of man, a form that was a physical light-body, participating still in the forces of the light. Because of the refinement of this body there could descend into it not only an etheric and an astral body, not only the ego in its first beginnings, but also the higher spiritual beings who were connected with the earth. Man was, as it were, rooted above in the divine spiritual beings, and these permeated him. It is really not

53

easy to portray the splendor of the earth at that time. We must picture it as a light-filled globe, shone round by light-bearing clouds and generating wonderful phenomena of light and color. Had one been able to feel this earth with his hands, he would have perceived warmth-phenomena. The luminous masses surged back and forth. Within them were all the human beings of today, woven through by all the spiritual beings, who rayed forth light in manifold grandeur and beauty. Outside was the earth-cosmos in its great variety; inside, with the light flowing about him, was man, in close connection with the divine-spiritual beings, raying streams of light into the outer light-sphere. As though by an umbilical cord that sprang from the divine, man hung upon this totality, on the light-womb, the world-womb of our earth. It was a collective world-womb in which the light-plant man lived at that time, feeling himself one with the light-mantle of the earth. In this refined vaporous plant-form, man hung as though on the umbilical cord of the earth-mother and he was cherished and nourished by the whole mother earth. As in a cruder sense the child of today is cherished and nourished in the maternal body, so the human germ was cherished and nourished at that time. Thus did man live in the primeval age of the earth.

Then the sun began to withdraw itself, taking the finest substances with it. There came a time when the high sun-beings forsook men, for all that today belongs to the sun forsook our earth and left the coarser substances behind. As a result of this departure of the sun, the mist cooled to water; and where there was formerly a mist-earth, now there was a water-sphere. In the middle were the primeval waters, but not surrounded by air; going outward, the waters changed into thick, heavy mist, which gradually became more refined. The earth of that time was a water-earth. It contained various materials in a soft state, which were enveloped by mists that became ever finer until, in the highest spheres, they became extremely rarefied. Thus did our earth once appear and thus was it altered. Men had to sink the formerly luminous gas-form into the turbid waters and incarnate there as shaped water-masses swimming in the water, as previously they had been air-forms floating in the air. Man became a water-form, but not entirely. Never did man descend entirely into the water.

This is an important moment. It has been described how the earth was a water-earth, but man was only partially a water-being. He protruded into the mist-sheath, so that he was half a water, half a vapor-being. Below, in the water, man could not be reached by the sun; the water-mass was so thick that the sunlight could not penetrate it. The light of the sun could penetrate into the vapor to some extent, so that man dwelt partly in the dark light-deprived water and partly in the light-permeated vapor. Of one thing, however, the water was not deprived, and this we must describe more minutely.

From the beginning, the earth was not only glowing and shining, but was also resounding, and the tone had remained in the earth, so that when the light departed the water became dark, but also became drenched with tone. It was the tone that gave form to the water, as one may learn from the well-known experiment in physics. We see that tone is something formative, a shaping force, since through tone the parts are arranged in order. Tone is a shaping power, and it was this that formed the body out of the water. That was the force of tone, which had remained in the earth. It was tone, it was the sound that rings through the earth, out of which the human form shaped itself. The light could reach only to the part of man that protruded out of the water. Below was a water-body; above was a vapor-body, which the external light touched, and which, in this light, was accessible to the beings who had gone out with the sun. Formerly, when the sun was still united with the earth, man felt himself to be in their womb. Now they shone down on him in the light and irradiated him with their power.

We must not forget, however, that in what remained behind after the separation of the sun other forces, the Moon-forces, were present. The earth had to separate these forces from itself.

Here we have a period during which only the sun was withdrawn, when the plant-man had to descend gradually into the water-earth. This stage, at which man had then arrived in his body, we see preserved today in a degenerated form in fishes. The fishes that we see in the water today are relics of those men, although naturally in a decadent form. We must think of a goldfish, for example, in a fantastic plant-form, agile, but with a feeling of sadness because the light had been withdrawn from the water. It was a very deep longing that arose. The light was no longer there, but the desire for the light called up this longing. There was a moment in the earth's evolution when the sun was not yet entirely outside the earth; there one can see that form still permeated with light—man with his upper part still at the sun-stage, while below he is already in the shape preserved in the fishes.

Through the fact that man lived in darkness with half his being, he had in his lower parts a baser nature, for in the submerged parts he had the Moon-forces. This part was not petrified like lava, as in the present moon, but these were dark forces. Only the worst parts of the astral could penetrate here. Above was a vapor-form, resembling the head parts, into which the light shone from outside and gave him form. So man consisted of a lower and an upper part. Swimming and floating, he moved about in the vaporous atmosphere. This thick atmosphere of the earth was not yet air; it was vapor, and the sun could not penetrate it. Warmth could penetrate, but not light. The sun-rays could not kiss the whole earth, but only its surface; the earth-ocean remained dark. In this ocean were the forces that later went out as the moon.

As the light-forces penetrated into the earth, so also did the gods penetrate. Thus we have, below, the godless, god-deserted mantle of waters, permeated only by the force of tone, and, all around this, the vapor, into which extended the forces of the sun. Therefore in this vapor-body, which rose above the surface of the water, man still participated in what streamed to him as light and love from the spiritual world. But why did the world of tone permeate the dark watery core? Because one of the high sun-spirits had remained behind, binding his existence to the earth. This is the same spirit whom we know as Yahveh or Jehovah.

Yahveh alone remained with the earth, sacrificing himself. It was he whose inner being resounded through the water-earth as shaping tone.

But since the worst forces had remained as the ingredients of the water-earth, and since these forces were dreadful elements, man's vapor-portion was drawn ever further down, and out of the earlier plant-form a being gradually evolved that stood at the stage of the amphibian. In saga and myth this form, which stood far below later humanity, is described as the dragon, the human amphibian, the lindworm. Man's other part, which was a citizen of the realm of light, is presented as a being which cannot descend, which fights the lower nature; for example, as Michael, the dragon-slayer, or as Saint George combating the dragon. Even in the figure of Siegfried with the dragon, although transformed, we have pictures of man's rudiments in their primeval duality. Warmth penetrated into the upper part of the earth and into the upper part of physical man, and formed something like a fiery dragon. But above that rose the ether body, in which the sun's force was preserved. Thus we have a form that the Old Testament well describes as the tempting serpent, which is also an amphibian.

The time was now approaching during which the basest forces were hurled out. Mighty catastrophes shook the earth, and for the occultist the basalt formations appear as remnants of the cleansing forces that rocked the globe when the moon had to separate from the earth. This was also the time when the water-core of the earth condensed more and more, and the firm mineral kernel gradually evolved. On the one hand, the earth grew denser through the departure of the moon; on the other, the upper parts gave off their heavier, coarser substances to the lower. Above, there arose something which, although still permeated by water, became more and more similar to our air. The earth gradually acquired a firm kernel in the middle, around which was the water everywhere. At first, the mist was still impenetrable for the sun's rays, but by relinquishing its substances the mist grew thinner and thinner. Later, much later, air developed out of this, and gradually the sun's rays, which earlier could not reach the earth itself, were able to penetrate it.

Now came a stage that we must picture correctly. Earlier, man dived down into the water and extended up into the mist. Now, through the condensation of the earth, the water-man slowly acquired the possibility of solidifying his form and taking on a hard bony system. Man hardened himself within himself. Thereby he transformed his upper part in such a way that it became suited for something new. This new thing, which previously was impossible, was the breathing of air. Now we find the first beginning of the lungs. In the upper part there has previously been something that took up the light, but could do nothing more. Now man felt the light again in his dull consciousness. He could feel what streamed down in it as divine forces coming toward him. In this transitional stage man felt that what streamed down upon him was divided into two parts. The *air* penetrated into him as breath. Previously only the *light* had reached him, but now the air was inside him. Feeling this, man had to say to himself, "Formerly I felt that the force that is above me gave me what I now use for breathing. The light was my breath."

What now streamed into him appeared to man as two brothers. Light and air were two brothers for him; they had become a duality for him. The earthly breath that streamed into man was at the same time an annunciation that he had to learn to feel something entirely new: As long as there was light alone, he did not know birth and death. The light-permeated cloud transformed itself perpetually, but man felt this only as the changing of a garment. He did not feel that he was born or that he died. He felt that he was eternal, and that birth and death were only episodes. With the first drawing of breath, the consciousness of birth and death entered into him. He felt that the air-breath, which had split off from its brother the light-ray, and which thereby had split off also the beings who earlier had flowed in with the light, had brought death to him.

Formerly, man had the consciousness, "I have a dark form, but I am connected with the eternal being." Who was it that destroyed

58

this consciousness? It was the air-breath that entered into man—Typhon. Typhon is the name of the air-breath. When the Egyptian soul experienced within itself how the formerly united stream divided itself into light and air, the cosmic event became a symbolic picture for this soul—the murder of Osiris by Typhon, or Set, the air-breath.

A mighty cosmic event is hidden in the Egyptian myth that allows Osiris to be killed by Typhon.* The Egyptian experienced the god who came from the sun and was still in harmony with his brother, as Osiris. Typhon was the air-breath that had brought mortality to man. Here we see one of the most pregnant examples of how the facts of cosmic evolution repeat themselves in man's inner knowledge.

In this way the trinity of sun, moon, and earth came into being. All of this was communicated to the Egyptian pupil in deep and consciously formed pictures.

* Fairly complete versions of this myth may be found in Padraic Colum: *Orpheus Myths of the World* (New York, Macmillan, 1930) and in Lewis Spence: *Mysteries of Egypt* (London, Rider & Co., 1929).

LECTURE 6

The Influence of Osiris and Isis.
Facts of Occult Anatomy and Physiology.

September 8, 1908

MANY of you, in reflecting upon what we have said in the last few days about the evolution of the earth and the solar system in relation to man, will have encountered what seems to you a curious contradiction of many present-day highly prized notions. You will have said to yourselves, "Yesterday we heard that the worst forces in evolution were connected with the moon, that when the moon separated from the earth the worst forces went out with it, and that only through this did the earth achieve a condition in which man could pursue his evolution. When we hear all this, what about the romantic aspect of the moon, what about all the poetry that speaks with such true feeling of the moon's wonderful influences upon man?"

This is only an apparent contradiction. It is resolved if we do not regard the facts onesidedly, if we place the whole complex of facts before our souls. It is certainly true that if we examined the physical mass of the moon we would find that it was not fitted to support life as we know it here on earth. We must also say that everything of an etheric nature that is connected with the moon and its physical substances appears in large part inferior, even decadent, when compared with the etheric in our own corporeality. Furthermore, if we should observe the astral nature of the individual moon-beings clairvoyantly—and we are entirely justified in speaking of them—we would be convinced that the worst and basest feelings that we have on earth are as nothing compared to what is found on the moon. Thus, in respect of the astral, the etheric, and the physical parts of the moon, we may speak of beings, of elements, that had to be expelled so that our earth could pursue its way, free from injurious influences.

But now we must recognize another fact. We must not forget that we cannot simply stop with what is base or evil, for everything that becomes base or evil in evolution is subject to a significant fact. As long as this is at all possible, everything that has sunk deep down into lower spheres must be purified through other, more perfect beings, must be raised up and purged, so that it may again be used in the economy of the universe. If we find a place in the cosmos where especially base beings congregate, we may be sure that with these baser beings are connected other higher ones, who have so great a power for the good, the beautiful, and the noble that they are fitted to lead even the lowest forces toward the good. It is true that all the basest things are connected with the moon's existence, but on the other hand, very high beings also are connected with it. We already know, for example, that the high spiritual personality of Yahveh dwells on the moon. So exalted a being, possessed of such power and glory, has under him vast hosts of ministering beings of a benevolent nature. We must understand that, although the basest forces departed from the earth with the moon, there also remained connected with the moon certain beings who are capable of transforming the bad into good, the ugly into beauty. They could not have done this had they left the ugly in the earth; they had to withdraw it.

But why did evil and ugliness have to come into existence

61

at all? They had to come into existence because without them something else would never have come to birth. Man would never have been able to become a self-forming, self-contained being.

Let us recall the foregoing lecture. There we saw how man's lower nature was rooted in the water, how he was half sunk in the dark water-earth. There were no bones at that time, no firm human shape. There was a flower-like form, which perpetually metamorphosed itself. Man would have remained like this if the forces had not developed further under the influence of the moon. Had the earth remained exposed to the sun alone, the mobility of the human form would have been enhanced to the highest degree. The earth would have attained a tempo impossible for man, and man would never have been able to develop his present form. On the other hand, if only the moon forces had been influential, man would have rigidified immediately; his form would have been frozen at the moment of birth; he would have become a mummy. Today man evolves between these two extremes, between unlimited mobility and complete rigidity. Because the forming forces are in the moon, the physical moon has become slag. Only the exalted and powerful beings who are connected with the moon can extend their influence into these forms.

Thus two types of forces influence the earth; the sun-forces and the moon-forces, the one stimulating and the other mummifying. Let us imagine that a giant steals the sun away. In that moment we would all become stiff like mummies, so stiff that we would never again be able to lose this form. But if the giant took the moon away, all the beautiful measured movements that we have today would become convulsive. We would become inwardly entirely mobile; we would see our hands prolong themselves to the gigantic, and then shrink up again. The power of metamorphosis would be vastly intensified. Now, however, man is inserted between these two forces.

Within this cosmos, many things are wisely arranged, not only in the various forms and substances but in the relations of things to each other. In order to bring this endless wisdom before our souls we shall now consider a relationship associated with the figure of Osiris.

In the figure of Osiris, the Egyptian saw the influence of the sun upon the earth in the time when mists and vapors still covered the earth, when there was still no air, and he saw that when breathing began in man, the unitary being, Osiris-Set, split. Set or Typhon caused the breath to enter into us. Typhon separated himself from the light of the sun, while Osiris worked only as the light of the sun. But this is also the moment when birth and death entered into the being of man. Into what was forming and unforming, which was previously like putting on and taking off a garment, a great change had entered. If man had been able to experience the effects of those high beings who later went out from the earth with the sun in the time when the influences proceeding from the sun had not yet left the earth, he would have looked up with thankfulness to these sun-beings. But as the sun separated itself from the earth more and more, and as the vapor-sphere—which for man at that time was the realm of his higher nature—refined itself more and more, then man, who was able to perceive the direct influence of the sun less and less, acquired the consciousness of what the forces in his lower nature were, and he came to the point of grasping his ego there. When he dived down into his lower nature, he became conscious of himself for the first time.

Why has the being whom we know as Osiris become darkened? The light ceased to work when the sun departed, but Yahveh remained with the earth until the moon split off. Osiris was the spirit who contained the force of the sunlight in such a way that, when the moon later departed, he accompanied it and received the task of reflecting the sunlight from the moon to the earth. Thus at first we see the sun depart; Yahveh remains behind on earth with his hosts, with Osiris. Man learns to breathe, and at the same time the moon departs. Osiris withdraws with the moon and is given the task of reflecting the sunlight from the moon to the earth. Osiris is laid into a chest, i.e., he withdraws with the

63

moon. Until this time man had received the Osiris-influence from the sun. At this point he begins to feel that what previously came to him from the sun now streams down upon him from the moon. Man said to himself when the moon shone down, "Osiris, it is you who from the moon send me the light of the sun, which belongs to your nature."

But this light of the sun is reflected in a different form every day. We have the first form when the moon appears as a tiny crescent in the heavens. On the next day it has grown to the second form, and so on through fourteen days until we have the fourteenth form in the full moon. In fourteen days Osiris turns himself toward the earth in the fourteen forms of the illuminated moon-disk. It is of deep significance that the moon, i.e., Osiris, takes on fourteen forms, fourteen phases of growth, in order to guide the light of the sun to us. In the cosmos this activity of the moon is connected with the concurrent fact that man has learned to breathe. Only when this phenomenon was fully established in the heavens was man able to breathe. Thereby he was attached to the physical world, and the first germ of the ego could originate in the being of man.

The later Egyptian knowledge felt all that has been described here, and recounted it by saying, "Osiris ruled the earth in past times. Then arose Typhon, the wind. (This is the time when the waters sink so far that the air appears, through which man becomes an air-breather.) Typhon overcame the Osiris-consciousness, killed Osiris, laid him in a chest, and committed him to the sea."

How could the cosmic event be better described in a picture? First, the sun-god Osiris reigns, then he is driven out with the moon. The moon is the chest that is pushed out into the ocean of cosmic space; thereafter Osiris is in cosmic space. But we recall that in the myth it is told that when Osiris was found again, when he arose again in cosmic space, he appeared in fourteen forms. The myth says that Osiris was cut into fourteen pieces and was buried in fourteen graves. Here in this profound myth we have a wonderful reference to the cosmic event. The fourteen aspects

of the moon are the fourteen pieces of the dismembered Osiris.*
The complete Osiris is the whole moon-disk.

At first this appears as though it were all only a symbol. But
we shall see that it had a real significance. Now we come to
something without which the mysteries of the cosmos will never
be clear to us. If such a constellation of sun, moon, and earth
had not arisen, if the moon had not appeared in fourteen aspects,
then something else could not have arisen, for these fourteen
aspects caused something special. Each of them has had a great
and powerful influence on man in his evolution on earth. Now I
must tell you something that is strange, but true.

At the time when all this had not yet happened, when Osiris
had not yet withdrawn, man in his light-form did not have the
foundation for something that today is of the greatest importance.
We know that the spinal cord is important. The nerves proceed
from it. Not even the beginnings of these were present in the
time when the moon had not yet departed. These fourteen aspects
of the moon, in the order in which they follow on one another,
were the cause of fourteen nerve-filaments being annexed to the
human spinal cord. The cosmic forces worked in such a way
that these fourteen nerve-filaments correspond to the fourteen
phases or aspects of the moon. This is the result of the Osiris
influence. But something else also corresponds to the moon-
evolution. These fourteen phases are only half the phenomena of
the moon. The moon has fourteen phases from new moon to full
moon, and fourteen phases from full moon to new moon. During
the fourteen days leading to the new moon, there is no Osiris
influence. Then the sun shines upon the moon in such a way that
the latter gradually turns its unilluminated surface to the earth
as the new moon. These fourteen phases from full moon to new
also have their result, and for the Egyptian consciousness this
result was achieved through Isis. These fourteen phases are ruled
by Isis. Through the Isis influence fourteen other nerve-filaments
proceed from the spinal cord. This makes a total of twenty-eight

* For confirming material see E. A. Wallis Budge: *Osiris and the
Egyptian Resurrection* (London, P. L. Warner, 1911), pp. 19–21.

nerve-filaments, corresponding to the different phases of the moon. So we see, from the viewpoint of cosmic events, the origin of specific members of the human organism.

Many will now object that this does not account for all the nerves, but only for twenty-eight of them.* There would have been only twenty-eight had the moon-year coincided with the sun-year. But the sun-year is longer, and the difference between the two caused the surplus nerves. Thus from the moon the influences of Isis and Osiris were built into the human organism. But something further is connected with this.

Up to the moment when the moon began to work from outside, there had been no duality of sex. There had been only a human being who was both male and female. The division occurred first through the alternating influences of Isis and Osiris from the moon. Whether a person became male or female depended upon whether the Osiris nerves or the Isis nerves exercised a certain influence on the organism. An organism in which the Isis influence predominated was male, whereas a body in which the Osiris influence prevailed became female. Naturally, both forces, Isis and Osiris, work in every man and in every woman, but in such a way that in men the etheric body is female, while in women it is male. Here we have something of the wonderful connection between the single being and the situation in the cosmos.

We have seen that man is influenced not only through the forces but also through the constellations, or positions, of the heavenly bodies. All that belongs to the male or female organisms formed itself under the influence of these twenty-eight nerves proceeding from the spinal cord. Now we will bring forward something that will give an insight into the cosmos and its connections with human evolution. These forces form the human shape, but man does not rigidify in it; an equilibrium is achieved between sun and moon influences. In the following, we must not think that we are dealing with mere symbols; it is solid facts that concern us.

What is the original Osiris, the undismembered Osiris? What

* There are generally thirty-one pairs of spinal nerves.

is the divided Osiris? What previously was a unity in man is now divided into the twenty-eight nerves. We have seen how in ourselves he lies dismembered. Without this, the human form could never have come into being. What formed itself under the influence of the sun and moon? Through the joint working of all the nerves there was brought into being, not only the externally male and female, but also within man something arose through the influence of the male and female principles. There arose the inner Isis-result, and this is the lungs. The lungs are the regulator of the influences of Typhon or Set. What works on man from Osiris, by stimulating the female influence in a masculine way, causes the lungs to be made productive through the breath. Through the influences that proceed from sun and moon, the masculine and feminine principles are regulated: in every female, something masculine—the larynx; in every male, something feminine—the lungs.

Isis and Osiris work inwardly in every person, in respect to his higher nature. Thus every person is double-sexed, having both lungs and larynx. Every person, whether man or woman, has the same number of nerves.

After Isis and Osiris had thus torn themselves out of the lower nature, they bore the son, the creator of the future earth-man. Together they produced Horus. Isis and Osiris begot the child, which was sheltered and nurtured by Isis: the human heart, sheltered and nurtured by the lung-wings of Mother Isis. Here in this Egyptian image we have something that shows us that in these ancient mystery-schools what had become the higher nature of man was looked upon as male-female, which is what the Indian recognized as Brahma. The Indian pupil was shown, in the original man, what later appears as that loftier form. Horus the child was shown to him, and he was told that all this had arisen through the primeval sound, through the Vach, the primeval sound that differentiates itself into many sounds.

What the Indian pupil experienced has been preserved for us in a remarkable verse in the Rigveda. In this is a passage that says, "And there come over man the seven from below, the eight from above, the nine from behind, the ten from out the foundations of the rocky vault, and the ten from within, while the mother cares for the suckling child." This is a remarkable passage. Let us imagine Isis, whom I described as the lungs, and Osiris, whom I described as the breathing-apparatus, and let us think how the voice works into this, differentiating itself into throat-sounds, lung-sounds, as in the letters of the alphabet. These letters come from different sides; seven come from below out of the throat, and so on. The singular working of everything connected with our air-apparatus is shown here. The place where the sound differentiates and divides is the higher mother, who fosters and nurses the child: the mother—the lungs; the child—the human heart, which is molded by all the influences, and from which come impulses to ensoul the voice.

Thus the mysterious working and weaving within the cosmos was revealed to the neophyte. Thus it built itself up in the course of time, and we shall see how the other members of man built themselves into this web. In this Egyptian occult teaching we have a chapter of occult anatomy as this was cultivated in an Egyptian mystery-school, insofar as man had knowledge of cosmic forces, of cosmic beings, and their connection with the human physical body.

LECTURE 7

Evolutionary Events in the Human
Organism up to the Departure
of the Moon.
Osiris and Isis as Builders of the
Upper Human Form.

September 9, 1908

IN the preceding lectures we have brought before our eyes, in connection with the nature of man, a long series of facts related to the evolution of the earth and of the whole solar system. In the last two lectures we directed our particular attention to bringing forward those facts of the evolution of sun, moon, and earth which had a sort of resurrection in the Egyptian mysteries, and which the pupil of these mysteries, as well as the whole Egyptian people, learned to know. In his clairvoyant seeing the pupil actually learned to know all the things mentioned here, as well as those that will be brought out today.

The greater part of the people, who were unable to raise themselves to clairvoyance, learned about all this in a most significant picture. We have often touched upon this picture, which was the most important one in the Egyptian world-view. It is embodied in the myth of Isis and Osiris. We are all acquainted with this picture, and no one who knows anything believes that it is without significance.* It was not only a picture for these people, but it was much more. What was contained in the Isis myth was told approximately as follows.

In earlier times Osiris long ruled the earth, to the blessing of humanity. This continued up to a particular moment, later characterized as the point when the sun stood in the sign of the Scorpion. Then it was that Typhon, or Set, killed his brother Osiris by inducing him to lay himself down in a chest, which Typhon then closed and committed to the sea. Isis, the sister and wife of Osiris, searched for her brother and husband, and after finding him brought him to Egypt. But the evil Typhon, still striving for the destruction of Osiris, cut him in pieces. Isis gathered the fragments together and buried them in various places. (Various graves of Osiris are still shown in Egypt.) Then Isis bore Horus, who avenged his father on Typhon. Osiris was now again admitted into the world of the divine spiritual beings and is no longer active on earth, but he aids men when they sojourn in the spiritual world between death and a new birth. Therefore in Egypt the path of the dead was called the way to Osiris.

This is the myth, which is one of the most ancient components of the Egyptian conception of life. Although there were later additions and changes, this legend pervaded all the cults of Egypt as long as any life remained in the Egyptian religious views.

Having directed our attention to this myth, into which was compressed what the pupil saw as a real event in the holy secrets of the mystery schools, we must now turn our attention to what we began yesterday and try to gain a clearer understanding of what was produced in man through the influence of the various aspects of the moon. We have spoken of the twenty-eight nerves proceeding from the spinal cord, which stem from the positions of the moon during the twenty-eight days that the moon requires to return to its first form. We have probed the mystery of how,

* In classical antiquity this feeling of baffling importance was already present. See Plutarch, *On Isis and Osiris.*

through the cosmic forces, these twenty-eight pairs of nerves were formed in man from outside. Now I beg you to heed well the following.

So far as possible in a short discourse, we shall now describe, as precisely as possible, what the Egyptian pupil learned about human evolution in a still broader sense. Those who are too strongly infected by modern anatomy will say that this description is pure nonsense from the contemporary point of view. They may say this, but they should be aware that this is the doctrine that the Egyptian neophyte not only learned, but clairvoyantly observed. I shall speak to those who are perceptive enough to be able to follow. This teaching was not only the result of the vision of the Egyptian in the mysteries, but it is also accepted as true by the modern occultist of today.

Let us recall what was said in the last lectures about how the earth, while still at the beginning of its evolution, consisted entirely of human germs, which formed the primeval earth-mist. The Indian clairvoyant, as well as the Egyptian, could see the entire subsequent human form sprout forth spiritually out of this spiritual human germ. All that later grew out of this human germ could be seen clairvoyantly at that time. But one could also look back on those parts of man that first arose out of the germ. The first that arose out of this germ, when the sun was still connected with the earth, was actually like a sort of plant, which opened its chalice upward. These forms filled, so to say, the whole earth as they shaped themselves out of the primeval mist. But in the earliest time in which this arose, like a sort of flower corolla opening itself into cosmic space, this corolla was scarcely visible; man would only have been able to perceive it by feeling its presence as a chalice-shaped warmth-body. This was present at first as a warmth-body. While the earth was still connected with the sun, the inner part of this human formation began to light up and to shine into cosmic space. If at that time one had been able to see with the eyes of today, on approaching such a light-form one would have seen a sparkling sphere, like a glittering sun, which cast its gleams into space in a regular form.

71

Today, one can hardly form a clear picture of what existed at that time. This would only be possible if one could conceive of the pure atmosphere of our earth as completely filled with fire-flies raying their light out into cosmic space. Thus would the first beginnings of man have shone into cosmic space when the earth was still connected with the sun. But this was not all that existed. At about the same time a sort of gas-body took form, outside and around the chalice form. Many substances were present in this, in solution, just as today we find fluid and solid substances in the human and animal bodies. At that time, how-ever, they were air-forms. Soon after all this had arisen, other germs came out of the common earth-mass, germs that were the first indications of our present animal kingdom. Thus the human kingdom came forth first; then came the germs that gave rise to the animal kingdom. The earth still consisted of an air-mass, of gleaming light-disseminating bodies, which shone into cosmic space. Within this air-mass emerged the first traces of sexless animals, which stood at the lowest stage of the present animal kingdom. We shall see that these animals, then arising in their first outlines, had a certain significance for man.

The important thing is that these animals, which then made their appearance, composed the thickest of the gas-masses, like thick clots of gas. These animals deveolped through most diverse forms to a certain level, and when the sun had just gone forth from the earth, the highest animal form was the fish, although not the fish of today. The form of the animals of that time was entirely different from that of the present fishes, but it stood at the same stage. In the course of evolution our fishes have retained what could be achieved while the sun was still in the earth. Now the earth condensed to a water-earth and the densest forms, the animals, swam in this water-earth. Something singular now came about. Certain of the primitive fish-forms remained animals and troubled themselves no further about the progress of evolu-tion. Others, however, retained a certain relation to the human shapes in the following way.

At the same time that the sun went out from the earth, the

earth began to turn on its axis so that at one time one side of the earth would be shone upon by the sun, and at another time it would not be shone upon; thus day and night began. But at that time, the days and nights were much longer than today. At the time when the moon had not yet split off, whenever such a human form (already considerably condensed) was on the sunny side, there was organized into this gas-mass something of such an animal form below in the water-earth. Human and animal forms were combined so that there was a human form above and an animal form below. The upper part protruded toward the sun, but the lower parts were weaker, and the animal body joined itself to them. The upper part protruded out of the water-earth, and the sun influence, proceeding through the flower-men, worked on the inner forces of earth and moon. Because here an animal form was joined to the human body, which was then at the fish level, it was said that the sun, which illuminated the human body, stood at the sign of the Fish. The first hint of this formation actually coincided with the sun's being in the sign of the Fish, but the sun passed many times through this sign before the next formation took place. The beginning of this formation, however, was the time when the sun stood in the zodiacal sign of the Fish, and this sign received its name because beings at the fish stage united themselves with man at that time.

Now, as we know, evolution proceeded in such a way that moon and earth formed one body. At the separation of the sun, Yahveh remained with the earth along with the moon forces, and among his ministers was the godly form the Egyptians called Osiris. Until the moon left the earth, evolution proceeded in a strange way.

We know that the earth was a water-earth, and the formation in the water attained an ever lower stage during the time preceding the departure of the moon. When the moon withdrew, man's lower nature was at about the stage of a great amphibian. This is what the Bible calls the serpent, and what is elsewhere called the lindworm or dragon. During the time when the moon was withdrawing, more and more of the animal kingdom had worked

73

itself into the lower human form. When the moon finally left, man had a hideous animal-like form in his lower parts, although above he still had the last remnants of a light-form into which the forces of the sun flowed from without. It was still possible for the light-beings to work into man. He moved about in the primal ocean, floating and swimming, with this remarkable light-form protruding out of the water-earth. What was this light-form? In the course of time it had transformed itself into a powerful and comprehensive sense-organ. When the moon withdrew, this transformation was complete. When man swam in the primal ocean, if some dangerous being approached him, he could perceive it with this organ. Especially could warmth and cold be perceived with it. This organ later shrivelled up, so that today it is the so-called pineal gland. At that time man moved within the earth-mass, floating and swimming, using this organ as a sort of lantern. In very young children we still find a soft place in the head, and it was from there that this organ protruded into cosmic space.

There were ever higher animal forms, which man took into himself. At one time, what had developed out of the fish was called the Water-man, because it lived in the water and contained the germ of the later man. A still higher form that developed could be called the Goat. The singular thing is that what corresponded to man in his lower members actually gave the name to the then prevailing constellation. The feet are actually the original Fish; the calves or shanks are the Water-man, which for a long time enabled man to steer while swimming; the knee we find to be related to the sign of the Goat. The animal kingdom evolved more and more, and what became the thigh was designated as the Archer. It would lead too far if I attempted to explain this expression, but we shall try to give a picture of how man looked when the animal kingdom corresponded to the Archer.

Man was an animal then, which for the first time could move about on the islands that were forming in the water. In his upper parts he became ever finer, and at the top he actually preserved the flower-form. He was illuminated from above by an organ that he carried on his head like a lantern. The then human form is rightly conceived if we see the upper part as etheric and the lower part as animal-like. In older pictures of the Zodiac, the form of the Archer is shown as an animal below and a man above. These signs portray the stage of evolution at which man then stood, even as the centaur reflects an actual stage of evolution—upward man and downward horse. The horse must not be taken literally, but as a representative of the animal kingdom. This was the artistic principle in earlier times; the artist portrayed what the clairvoyant described to him or what he himself had seen. Artists were often initiates. It is said that Homer was a blind seer, but that means that he was clairvoyant. He could look back into the Akashic Record. Homer, the blind seer, was much more seeing in the spiritual sense than were the other Greeks. Thus, the centaur was once an actual human form. When man looked like this, the moon had not yet withdrawn. The moon force was still in the earth, and in man was still what had formed itself during the sun period, the shining pineal gland, which he bore like a lantern on his head.

When the moon withdrew from the earth, sexuality appeared. The centaur-man was still sexless. Sexuality appeared when the sun stood in the sign of the Scorpion, and this is why we always connect sex with this sign. The Scorpion is what in the animal kingdom corresponds to the stage of evolution at which man stood when he had developed sexuality. In his upper half, man was turned toward the cosmic forces, but in his lower half he was a bisexual being. He had become a sexual being. When the clairvoyant pupil of the Egyptian mysteries directed his gaze toward this period of earth-evolution, he saw the earth peopled by men whose lower bodily form was becoming denser, in harmony with their baser nature, but who had a luminous human shape above.

Then began the time when, through the forces of the moon, the nerve-filaments appeared in the region where the spine now is. The formation above the spine, the present head-region, had condensed and changed itself into the human brain; that was the completely transformed light-organ. Attached to this was the spine, from which the nerves proceeded, and attached to this in turn was the lower man whom we have described. This was revealed to the Egyptian pupil, and it became clear to him that any being wishing to incarnate on the earth would have to assume the corresponding human form. Osiris, as spirit, often visited the earth and incarnated as a man. Men felt that a god had descended, but he had a human form. Every exalted being who visited the earth appeared in the shape that man then had. This shape was then such that one still saw that light-body, that remarkable head-ornament, the lantern of Osiris,* which has been described in a pictorial way as the eye of Polyphemus. This is the organ, the lantern, which at first was outside the human body, and which then transformed itself into an inner organ in the brain. Everything in early art is a symbol of actual forms.

When the Greek initiates became acquainted with these mysteries of the Egyptians, they had already learned many things. Basically, they had learned the same things as the Egyptian initiates, but they gave them different names in their language. The initiates of the Egyptians had developed the clairvoyant gifts to a high degree, so that many of their pupils could look back clairvoyantly into those most ancient times. The Egyptian initiate had a direct connection with those mysteries, hence the Greek priests seemed to him to be only childish stammerers. This is illustrated by the words that an Egyptian priest once spoke to Solon, "O Solon, Solon, you Hellenes remain always children, and there is not an old man among you. In spirit you are all young; there is no old opinion handed down among you from ancient tradition, nor any science that is hoary with age." ** Thus did the Egyptian point out that his wisdom stood infinitely far above anything that can be experienced materially. Only in the Eleusinian mysteries did the Greeks progress equally far, but only a few participated in them.

* Pictures of this ornament may be found in E. A. Wallis Budge, *Osiris and the Egyptian Resurrection* (London, P. L. Warner, 1911), pages 42 and 49.
** See the opening passages of Plato's *Timaeus*.

In his study of earth-evolution, the Egyptian initiate saw that the god Osiris had separated himself from the sun and had gone to the moon, whence he reflected the light of the sun. What this god did was also sacred to the Greeks. They too knew that it was this god, Osiris, who formed the twenty-eight moon-aspects, and thereby laid the groundwork for the twenty-eight nerves in man. Through Osiris, the nervous system is built onto the spinal column, thereby forming the whole upper body of man. For what appears as muscle can maintain its form only because the nerves are its shapers. All we have as muscles, cartilage, and other organs such as heart and lungs, maintains its form only through the nerves. Thus through the earlier sun-activity appeared what took form as brain and spinal column, and on this spinal column the twenty-eight aspects of Isis and Osiris work from outside. Isis and Osiris are the shapers of all this, and in the tentacles that the brain sends down into the spinal column, Osiris works upon the spine. The Greeks experienced this also, and as they became acquainted with the Egyptian mysteries they recognized that Osiris was the same as the god whom they called Apollo. They said that the Egyptian Osiris was Apollo, and that, like Osiris, Apollo worked upon the nerves so as to achieve a soul-life within man.

Now in a simple way, let us try to view this formation. Let us think of the brain as it might be sketched. This continues itself into the spine, and there the twenty-eight arms of Osiris enter in; there Osiris with his twenty-eight hands plays upon the spine as upon a lyre. The Greeks had a significant image for this —the lyre of Apollo. We need only think of it as transposed. The lyre is the brain, the nerves are the strings on which the hands of Apollo play. Apollo plays on the cosmic-lyre, on the mighty work of art that the cosmos has formed, and that causes to resound in man the tones that compose his soul life. For the Eleusinian initiate, this was what the Egyptians had given in their pictures.

From such a picture we can see that these things should not be expounded too rigidly, or we shall merely be forcing fantasies into them. For as a rule, our experience should be that these pictures are actually much deeper than anything we can dream into them by means of the intellect. If the Greek clairvoyant spoke of Apollo, he had before his mind the mystery of Osiris-Apollo and the human musical instrument. Osiris stood before the Egyptian pupil when he was initiated into the mysteries of earth-existence. Thus we must say that these symbols, these pictures, which have been preserved for us and which characterize what has been taken from the primeval mysteries, mean much more than can be expounded by the intellect. This lyre was seen, the hands of Apollo were seen. The important thing is that we should relate every symbol to some actual vision, to something really seen. There are no symbols, no legends, that have not first been seen.

The Egyptian pupil could penetrate to such mysteries only after a long time. He was first prepared through a definite course of instruction, which was somewhat similar to basic theosophy. Then only was he admitted to the real exercises. There he experienced a sort of ecstatic condition which, although not yet true clairvoyance, was more than a dream. In this condition he beheld what he was later to see in the form of pictures. The pupil actually beheld in a mighty living dream the departure of the moon, and of Osiris with it, and Osiris's working upon the earth from the moon. He dreamed the Osiris-Isis legend. Every pupil dreamed this Osiris-Isis dream. He had to dream it, for otherwise he would not have been able to come to a perception of the true facts. The pupil had to go through the picture, the imagination. The legend of Isis and Osiris was inwardly experienced. This ecstatic soul-condition was a preliminary to the true vision, a prelude to his seeing what takes place in the spiritual world. What has been described today could be read by the pupil in the Akashic Record only when he had reached a high degree of initiation. Tomorrow we shall speak further of this, and also of the other signs of the Zodiac and their significance.

LECTURE 8

The Stages of Evolution of the Human Form.
The Expulsion of the Animal Beings.
The Four Human Types.

September 10, 1908

WE have become acquainted with significant events in the evolution of the human organism. We have followed this organism from its beginning to the point of time when the moon departed from the earth. When we say "point of time," we are not speaking literally, for these events occupied long periods. From the first moment when the moon began to show signs of withdrawing, until its departure had been completely accomplished, long stretches of time passed and many things occurred in evolution. But we have observed man until about the time of the departure of the moon. We have understood man's form which, as its lower part, approximately from the middle of the trunk to the height of the hips, manifested a configuration not entirely unlike his present shape. This body, although soft, could have been seen with modern eyes, whereas the upper parts were visible only to clairvoyant consciousness. We have already pointed out how something of man's nature at that time has been preserved by myth, religion, and art in the centaur. The various parts of the body, the members that gradually evolved into feet, shanks, knees, thighs, represent the animal forms of our earth at that time. These animal forms, however, remained stuck at certain stages of evolution, beyond which man was able to progress. Let us try to understand this thoroughly.

In the earliest times, when the sun departed, no animal forms had yet appeared. After the sun had left, the highest form of animal was a type that stood at the level of our present fish. When we say that the human feet corresponded to this fish-form, when we look at the feet in connection with fish, what does this mean? It means that the feet were the only part of man that was physically perceptible at the time when certain forms were left behind which swam about like fish in the water-earth. The remaining parts were present only in a finer etheric form. What we have described as the chalice or blossom form, the light-organ, was entirely etheric, an illuminated air-form. Only the lowest part of man was able really to wade through the water-earth like the fish that had remained behind.

Thereafter there were higher animals, which are depicted in the image of the Water-man, the man whose body was visible as high as the shanks. Man has been formed in such a way as to leave behind him, at every stage of his existence, certain animal forms, beyond which he slowly progressed. When the moon began to withdraw, man was so far along that he had given his lower half, his lower nature, a physical shape, whereas the upper half remained entirely pliable. Then, we see taking hold, from the moon, that influence of the moonlight which the Egyptians called Osiris, which can work upon man through the different aspects of the moon. We see how the most important formations of the upper body, i.e., the nerves that bring about the present upper body, are worked into man from the moon. The nerves, going out from the spine, formed the upper body. At first, through the tones that Osiris-Apollo played on the human lyre, the mid-part, the hip-region, comes into form. All that had to remain stuck at this point, beyond which man progressed, appears in later evolution in the forms of the amphibians.

As long as the moon was connected with the earth, it more or less pushed man's evolution down. The fish form was still connected with the sun, which is the reason for the feeling that every healthy person today has toward fish. Think of the pleasure of seeing a beautiful glittering fish, a shining water-animal, and then think of the antipathy one feels toward a frog, toad, or snake, although these stand higher than the fish. The forms of that time appear in their decadence as the present amphibians, but man once had such forms in his lower corporeality. As long as man had only a lower corporeality to the hips, he was a sort of dragon. It was only later, when the upper body assumed solid form, that by use of this he transformed the lower. We may say that the fish reflects the form that man possessed through the forces he received while the sun was still united with the earth. Until the sun departed, man stood at the level of the fish.

Now the great beings, the leaders of evolution, departed as they shaped their sun, to reunite with the earth only at a much later time. One of the Spirits, one who went out with the sun, the highest of the guiding Sun Spirits, was the Christ. We feel a deep reverence when we realize that up to this time man was united with this Being who, as the noblest spirit, once departed from the earth with the sun. One felt that through the form of the fish one could characterize the time of the sun's departure from the earth, and also the forms given through the Christ himself. Earlier, man on earth was united with the sun, and as the latter departed he saw, preserved in the fish-shape, the form that he owed to the sun spirits. As he progressed further, the sun spirits were no longer with him. The Christ departed from the earth when man still had the fish-shape. The initiates of the first Christian period preserved this form. In the Roman catacombs the fish appeared as the symbol of Christ, to remind men of the great cosmic event in evolution when the Christ was still united with them in the earth. Man had progressed to the fish-form when the sun split

81

off, and the first Christians felt a reference to the Man-Christ-form in the fish symbol as something of great profundity. Such a significant sign, which we view as a symbol of an epoch of cosmic evolution, is far removed from the external explanations that are often given. The true symbols refer to higher spiritual realities. They did not merely "mean" something to the early Christians. Such a symbol is a picture of this or that which one can really see in the spiritual world, and no symbol is rightly interpreted unless one can point to what can be seen in the spiritual world in connection with it. All speculation is at most preparatory, and the expression "it means" does not touch the point; for one first really understands the symbol when one shows how a spiritual fact is portrayed in it.

Now let us proceed further with the evolution of humanity. Man took on the most diverse forms, and when he had developed upward to the hip-level he was at his ugliest in his physical form. The shape he then had is preserved in a decadent form in the snake. The time when man had reached the amphibian form, when the moon was still in the earth, is the time of shame and degeneracy in the evolution of mankind. Had the moon not then departed from the earth, the race of men would have succumbed to a horrible fate, falling increasingly into evil forms. Hence the feeling that the naïve and unspoiled person has toward the snake, which retains the form that man had at his lowest point, is entirely justified. Precisely the unspoiled soul-attitude, which does not assert that there is nothing ugly in nature, feels a revulsion before the snake, because it is the document of human shame. This is not meant in a moral sense, but points to the lowest stage in human evolution.

Man had now to pass beyond this low point. He could do this only by abandoning the animal form and beginning to condense his spiritual upper part. We have seen that all the nobler parts could develop only through the intervention of the Isis and Osiris forces. In order for the Osiris forces to work in him, in order for the nobler part to develop, something important was necessary. Man's upper part had to find the possibility of bringing the spine out of the horizontal into the vertical. All this occurred through the influence of Isis and Osiris. Man was led from stage to stage by sun and moon, which kept themselves in balance. When half of man had become physical, sun and moon were in balance; therefore the hip region is designated as the Balance. At that time the sun was in the sign of the Balance.

Now we must not imagine—and this must be emphasized—that after the sun had stood in the sign of the Scorpion, and then in the sign of the Balance, the hips immediately developed. This would show the tempo of evolution as proceeding much too rapidly. The sun travels through the whole zodiac in a period of 25,920 years. At one time the sun rose in spring in the Ram, earlier in the sign of the Bull. The vernal point was always moving, going through the sign of the Bull, and so on. About 747 B.C. the sun again entered into the Ram; in our time it rises in the sign of the Fish. The time during which the sun traverses a sign has some significance, but such a period would not suffice for the change that had to take place in order for man to progress from sexuality under the sign of the Scorpion to the evolving of his hips under the sign of the Balance. We should have a false picture of this, if we thought that it could have occurred in *one* transit of the sun. The sun goes once through the zodiac, and only after this complete circuit does the forward step occur. In earlier times it had to make the transit oftener before the forward step could take place. Therefore we cannot apply to more ancient epochs the familiar time-reckonings of post-Atlantean times. The sun had first to go completely around—in earlier ages even several times—before evolution could progress a step. For those members that required a stronger molding, the time lasted even longer.

Man rises ever higher through this evolution. The next stage, during which the lower parts of the human trunk were formed, is designated by the sign of the Virgin.

We shall best understand evolution if we make it quite clear that, while man was becoming ever more human, animal beings remained stuck at certain stages. We have already said that man developed lungs, heart, and larynx through the influence of the moon forces. We have also shown to what extent Osiris and Isis participated in this. Now we must be quite clear that the higher organs, such as heart, lungs, larynx, and others, could develop only through the fact that the higher members of man— etheric body, astral body, and also the ego—cooperated in a definite way as the really spiritual members of man. After the point that was reached under the Balance, these higher members cooperated much more than in the preceding epochs. Thus the most manifold forms could appear. For example, the etheric body, or the astral, or the ego, could work especially strongly. It could even happen that the physical body might predominate over the other three members. Through this four human types developed. A number of men appeared who had worked out the physical body especially. Then there were men who had received their stamp from the etheric body, others whose astral nature predominated, and also ego-men, strongly marked ego-men. Each man showed what predominated in him. In the ancient times when these four forms originated, one could meet grotesque shapes, and the clairvoyant discovers what is present in the different types. There are representations, although these are not well known, in which the memory of this has been preserved. For example, those men in whom the physical nature became especially strong and worked on the upper parts, bore the mark of this in their upper part. Something was formed that was entirely suited to the baser form, and through what was thus active there appeared the shape that we see retained in the apocalyptic picture of the Bull, although not the bull of today, which is a decadent form. What was governed principally by the physical body at a certain time, remained stuck at the stage of the bull. This is represented by the bull and all that belongs to this genus, such as cows, oxen and so on. The human group in whom the etheric rather than the physical body was strongly marked, in whom the heart region was especially powerful, is also preserved in the animal kingdom. This stage, beyond which man has progressed, is preserved in the lion. The lion preserves the type that was worked out in the group of men in whom the etheric body was intensely active. The human stage in which the astral body overpowered the physical and etheric is preserved for us, although degenerated, in the mobile bird-kingdom, and is portrayed in the Apocalypse in the picture of the Eagle. The predominating astrality is here repelled; it raised itself from the earth as the race of birds. Where the ego grew strong, a being evolved that should actually be called a union of the three other natures, for the ego harmonizes all three members. In this group the clairvoyant actually has before him what has been preserved in the Sphinx, for the Sphinx has the lion-body, the eagle-wings, something of the bull form—and in the oldest portrayals there was even a reptilian tail, pointing to the ancient reptile form—and then at the front there is the human face, which harmonizes the other parts.

These are the four types. But in the Atlantean time the manform predominated, as the human shape gradually constructed itself out of the eagle, lion, and bull natures. These transmuted themselves into the full human form, and this gradually transmuted itself into the shape that was present in the middle of Atlantis. Something else occurred through all these events. Four different elements, four forms, merged harmoniously in man. One is present in the physical body, in the bull nature; these are the predominating forces that evolved up to the evolutionary period of the Balance. Then we have the lion nature in the etheric body; in the astral body, in the predominating forces of the astral, the eagle or vulture nature; finally, the predominating forces of the ego, the true human nature. In single beings, one or another of these members had the upper hand. Through this the four types arose. But one could meet still other combinations. For example, the physical, astral, and ego might be equal, while the etheric predominated; that is a particular type of mankind. Then there were beings in whom the etheric, astral, and ego had the upper hand, while the physical was less developed, so that we have men in whom the higher members prevail over the physical body. Those human beings in whom the physical, astral, and ego

85

predominated, are the physical ancestors of the males of today, while those in whom the etheric, astral, and ego predominated, are the physical ancestors of the females of today. The other types disappeared more and more; only these two remained, and evolved into the male and female forms.

How was it possible that gradually just these two forms evolved? This occurred through the differing effects of the working of the Isis and Osiris forces.

We have seen that in the phases of the new moon, when the moon is dark, Isis is characterized, but that Osiris is characterized in the shining phases of the full moon. Isis and Osiris are spiritual beings on the moon, but we find their deeds on the earth. We find them on the earth because it is through these deeds that the human race divided into two sexes. The female ancestors of human beings were formed through the influence of Osiris; the ancestors of men were formed through the workings of Isis. The influence of Isis and Osiris on mankind occurs through the nerve filaments, through the working of which mankind is developed into male and female. In the myth this is shown through Isis's seeking Osiris; the male and the female seek each other on the earth. Over and over again we see that wonderful events of cosmic evolution are hidden in these myths.

When the stage of the Balance had been passed, there gradually evolved in the upper members of the human being the differentiations we describe as male and female. Man remained unisexual much longer than the animals. What had long since occurred in the other animals now for the first time took place in man. There was a time when there was a unified human form, containing nothing of the method of propagation that later developed. During this time the nature of man contained both sexes in one being. "And God created man male-female," is the way it stands in the Bible, not "Male and female created he them." * He created both in one. It is the worst possible transla-

* Most texts are silent on this question, but the *International Critical Commentary* (New York, Scribner's, 1895), in discussing *Genesis* I:27, at least shows that others have entertained the male-female hypothesis. See

tion when we say, "Male and female created he them." This has no sense in face of the real facts.

Thus we look into a time when human nature was still a unity, when every person was virginally reproductive. This stage of evolution is portrayed in Egyptian traditions drawn from the vision of the initiates. I have already pointed out that the older representations of Isis were as follows: Isis is suckling Horus; but behind her stands a second Isis with vulture wings, who holds out the *Ankh* to Horus to indicate that man stems from a time when these types were still separate and that later the other astral being also sank down into man. This second Isis points to how the astral element predominated at one time. What was later united with the human form is here portrayed behind the mother, as the astral form that would have had vulture wings if it had followed only the astrality. But the time when the etheric body predominated is portrayed in a third Isis, lion-headed, behind the others. This threefold Isis is thus presented out of a deep vision.

From this point of view we shall also understand something else. There must have been a period of transition between unisexuality and the division into two sexes; there could have been an interim condition between the virginal propagation in which fructification occurred as a result of the forces living in the earth —which at the same time were fertilizing substances—and the other method of bisexual propagation. This bisexual propagation emerged completely only in the middle of the Atlantean epoch. Earlier there was an intermediate stage. At a certain epoch in this intermediate stage, a change of consciousness took place. Man then required much longer spans of time than today to go through an alternation of consciousness. That was a time in which consciousness was especially strong when, at night, man experienced himself as a spiritual being among his spiritual companions. Day-consciousness, on the other hand, was weak. This condition of consciousness changed in another period, when man's consciousness while in the physical body became strong,

---

also the curious remarks in the speech of Aristophanes in Plato's *Symposium*.

while his soul life became weaker upon leaving the physical plane at night.

Now there were times in human evolution in which we must recognize a transitional stage. Man's consciousness for the physical world was still damped down, and it was in this damped-down state that fructification occurred. In the periods of subdued consciousness, when man rose out of the physical world into the spiritual, fructification took place, and man noticed this only through a symbolical dream-act. In tender, noble fashion he felt that fertilization had occurred in his sleep, and in his consciousness there was only a delicate and wonderful dream; for example, that he threw a stone, that the stone fell into the earth, and that a flower rose out of the earth.

It is of special interest that in this time we have also to take into account those who had achieved this stage earlier. When we say that certain beings remained at the Bull stage, others at the Lion, others at the Eagle, and so on, what does this mean? It means that if these beings had been able to wait, if they could have developed their full love for the physical world only at a much later time, they would have become human beings. If the lion had not willed to enter into the earthly sphere too early, it would have become a man; the same is true of the other animals that had split off up till then. Let us repeat it in this way: All that was human at the time when the lion formed itself said either, "No, I will not yet take up the lower substances; I will not go down into physical humanity," or, "I will go down; I wish what has evolved to come into existence." Thus we must think of two beings. The one remains above in the etheric realm of the air and only in its earthly parts reaches down to earth, while the other strives to descend completely to the earth. The latter might become a lion; the former became a man. Just as the animals remained fixed at a certain stage, so now certain men remained fixed. It was not the best men who became human too early. The better ones were able to wait; they remained for a long time without descending to the earth and there carrying out the act of fructification consciously. They remained in that state of cognition in which this act of fructification was a dream.

One may say that these men lived in Paradise. We find that the men who descended earliest to earth had especially strongly formed bodies, with crude and brutal countenances; while the men who wished first to mold the nobler parts had a much more human form. What is here described was preserved in a wonderful myth and rite. The rite is mentioned by Tacitus* and is well known as the myth of the goddess Nerthus (Hertha), who descended every year into the sea in a boat. But those who drew the boat had to be killed. Nerthus is thought of (as is often done today) as a phantom of the imagination, as some kind of goddess to whom a cult had been dedicated on some island. It has been believed that the Nerthus shrine could be found in Lake Hertha on Rügen. It was thought that the place where the chariot sank might be found there. This is a remarkable fantasy. The name of Lake Hertha is a new invention. Earlier it was called the Black Lake because of its color, and it never occurred to anyone to call it Lake Hertha and relate it to the goddess.

There are much deeper things in this myth. Nerthus is the transitional stage between the virginal fructification and the later propagation. Nerthus, who dives down into a shadowy consciousness, perceives her immersion in the sea of passion only

* Tacitus's *Germania,* Section 40, reads in part as follows:
"On an island of the ocean is a holy grove, and in it a consecrated chariot, covered with robes. A single priest is permitted to touch it. He interprets the presence of the goddess in her shrine, and follows with deep reverence as she rides away drawn by cows. Then come days of rejoicing and all places keep holiday, as many as she thinks worthy to receive and entertain her. They make no war, take no arms; every weapon is put away; peace and quiet are then, and then only, known and loved, until the same priest returns the goddess to her temple, when she has her fill of the society of mortals. After this the chariot and the robes—if you are willing to credit it, the deity in person—are washed in a sequestered lake: slaves are the ministrants and are straightway swallowed by the same lake: hence a mysterious terror and an ignorance full of piety as to what that may be which men behold, only to die."

in a tender, symbolic act; she perceives only a reflection of it. But although the higher humanity still felt things in this way, those who had already descended at that time had lost their original naïveté. They already saw this act; they were lost for the higher human consciousness, and were worthy of death. The memory of this event of primeval times was preserved in rites in countless regions of Europe. A ceremony was carried out at certain times in commemorative festivals. This was the chariot of the Nerthus image, which dived down into the sea of passion, and it was the gruesome custom that those who had to serve, who drew the chariot and could see what went on, had to be slaves and were killed during the rite, as a sign that these were mortals who saw the act. Only the initiated priests could remain present during the ceremony without being harmed. From this example we see that in the time when what is here described was known in certain regions, the Nerthus cult existed. In these regions there was a consciousness that shaped this myth and the rite.

Thus mankind evolved through the most manifold forms, and thus what are real facts were presented in pictures. It has already been said that such pictures should not be regarded as allegories, that their content has a relation to the real facts. Such pictures arose like dreams. So the Osiris myth also was dreamed before the pupil could actually see the facts of human evolution, and only what prepares the way for real seeing is a symbol in the occult sense. A symbol is a description of real events in pictures. In the next lecture we shall discuss the effect of these descriptions.

LECTURE 9

The Influence of the Sun and
Moon Spirits, of the Isis
and Osiris Forces.
The Change in Consciousness.
The Conquest of the Physical Plane.

September 11, 1908

IN the preceding lectures we reviewed in some detail a number of facts concerning the evolution of humanity. I tried to
show how man developed in the period of evolution that stretches
approximately from the moment when the sun withdrew from
the earth to the time when the moon also departed. Today something will be added to these facts, which could be called "facts of
occult anatomy and physiology." In order to understand everything properly, however, today we must throw a little light on
certain other facts of the spiritual life, for we must not forget that
what is really to be demonstrated is the relation between the
Egyptian myths and mysteries, between the whole Egyptian cultural period, and our own time. Therefore it is necessary that we
be entirely clear about how evolution progressed further through
the various epochs.

Let us again recall what was described as the working of the
sun and moon spirits, especially of the Osiris and Isis forces,

through whose activities the human body first appeared and was built up. Remember that this occurred in the remote past, that our earth as yet had scarcely crystallized out of the water-earth, and that a great part of what was described actually took place in the water-earth. Man at that time was in a condition that we should bring clearly before our minds so that we may form a clear conception of how things looked to human vision during man's progress through evolution.

I have described how man's lower members, the feet, shanks, knees, etc., appeared as physical forms as early as the time when the sun had shown indications of withdrawing from the earth. But we must always remember what has been said so often: all this would have been visible had there been a human eye to see it. But such an eye did not exist. It appeared only much later. While man was still in the water-earth, he perceived only by means of the organ described as the pineal gland. Perception by means of the physical eye began only after the hip region had been formed. Thus we may say that man already had the lower part of the human form, but possessed nothing whereby he could have seen the body. At that time man could not see himself. Only at the moment when his body, building itself up from below, passed the region of the hips, did man receive the capacity of seeing himself. When he was shaped as far as the sign of the Balance, man's eyes were opened for the first time. Then he began to see himself as in a mist. Then he developed the vision of objects. Until the hip region evolved, all human perception, all seeing, was of a clairvoyant astral-etheric nature. At that time man could not yet see physical things. Human consciousness was still dark and shadowy, though of a dreamy clairvoyant nature.

Then man passed over to that condition of consciousness in which sleeping and waking alternated. When he was awake man saw darkly what was physical, but as though it were wrapped in mist and surrounded by an aura of light. In his sleep man rose to the spiritual worlds and the divine spiritual beings. He alternated between a clairvoyant consciousness, which grew ever weaker, and a day-consciousness, an object-consciousness, which grew stronger and stronger and is the head-consciousness of today. Gradually he lost the capacity of clairvoyant perception, together with the faculty of seeing the gods in sleep. However, the clarity of day-consciousness waxed in the same proportion, and the consciousness of self, the I-feeling, the I-perception, grew stronger.

If we look back into the Lemurian time, into the time before, during, and after the moon's exit from the earth, we find that man then had a clairvoyant consciousness in which he had no inkling of what we today call death. For if, at that time, man withdrew from his physical body, whether through sleep or through death, his consciousness did not diminish. On the contrary, he received a higher consciousness and, in certain ways, one more spiritual than his consciousness when in his physical body. He never said to himself, "Now I am dying," or, "I am falling into unconsciousness"—that did not exist in those times. Man did not yet rely on his own feeling of self, but he felt himself immortal in the womb of divinity, and for him all that we describe here today were obvious facts.

Let us imagine that we lie down to sleep, that the astral body removes itself from the physical, and that all this happens in the full moon. We have the physical and etheric bodies lying in bed, the astral body hovering above, and all of this in the full moonlight. Now the situation is not so that an astral cloud simply becomes visible there for the clairvoyant. On the contrary, what he actually sees is streams from the astral body into the physical, and these streams are the forces that remove fatigue in the night. They bring to the physical body replenishment for the wear and tear of the day, so that it feels refreshed and quickened. At the same time one would see spiritual streams proceeding from the moon, and these streams are permeated by astral powers. One would see how there actually proceed from the moon spiritual effects that permeate and strengthen the astral body and influence its working on the physical body.

Let us assume that we are men of the old Lemurian time.

Then the astral body would have perceived this streaming-in of the spiritual forces, would have gazed upward and said, "This is Osiris who strengthens me, who works on me. I see how his influence goes through me." We would have felt ourselves sheltered in Osiris during the night; we would have lived, so to say, in Osiris with our ego. We would have felt, "I and Osiris are one." Had we been able to give words to what we felt at that time, we would have described it approximately thus, when we returned into the physical body, "Now I must descend again into the physical body that waits for me there below; this is a time when I must dive down into my lower nature." We should have rejoiced when the time came when we could leave the physical body once again, and rise up to rest in the lap of Osiris, or in the lap of Isis, where we again united our ego with Osiris.

As the physical body evolved further, and especially after the development of the upper members, man could see more physically, could perceive the objects in the physical world about him. In the same proportion, however, he had to tarry longer when he descended into his physical body. He took more interest in the physical world. His consciousness grew darker for the spiritual world as his consciousness in the physical body became clearer. He became disaccustomed to the spiritual world. Thus the life of man in the physical world evolved further, and in the conditions that prevailed between death and a new birth consciousness grew darker and darker. In the Atlantean time man lost almost entirely the feeling of being at home with the gods, and when the great catastrophe was past, a great part of mankind had completely lost the natural ability to gaze into the spiritual world at night. But in place of this they gained the capacity of seeing ever more sharply by day, so that the objects around them appeared in ever clearer outlines. We have already pointed out that, among the men who had remained behind, the gift of clairvoyance was still preserved, even into the post-Atlantean cultures. At the time when Christianity was founded, remnants of this clairvoyance still existed, and even today there are occasional persons who have preserved it as a natural gift. But this clairvoyance is entirely different from that which is gained through esoteric training.

Thus night gradually grew dark for man in Atlantis, while day-consciousness began to light up. The night was without consciousness for the people of the first post-Atlantean culture, whom we tried to characterize in all their greatness, in the spirituality that entered through the holy Rishis. In the earlier lectures we examined these people, and now we must describe them from another side.

Let us try to enter into the souls of the pupils of the holy Rishis, into the souls of the people of the Indian culture in general, in the time immediately after the last traces of the great Atlantean water-catastrophes had vanished. A sort of memory of the ancient world still lived in the soul, a memory of that world in which man experienced and saw the gods who worked on his body, a memory of how Osiris and Isis worked on him. Now he had emerged from this world, out of the womb of the gods. Formerly all this had been present to him as the physical is present to him today. Like a memory this passed through the mind of the Indian man of the first post-Atlantean times, to whom the Rishis still could speak of how things actually had been. He knew that the Rishis and their pupils still could see into the spiritual world, but he also knew that for the normal person of the Indian culture the time was past when he could see into the spiritual world.

Like a painful memory of his old true home, this went through the soul of the ancient Indian when he saw himself transplanted into the physical world, which is only the outer shell of the spiritual world. He yearned to be out of this external world. He felt, "Unreal are the mountains and valleys, unreal the cloud-masses in the air, unreal even the firmament. All this is only like a sheath, like the physiognomy of a real being, and we cannot see the reality behind this, the gods and the true form of man. What we see is Maya, is unreal; the real is veiled." The feeling grew ever keener that man had sprung from the truth and had his real home in the spiritual; that the things of sense were untrue, were

Maya, and that the physical world of the senses was like night around him.* When one feels so strongly the contrast between the spiritual and the unreal physical, the religious mood will tend to produce little interest in the physical world and to lead the spirit toward what the initiates see, as to which the holy Rishis could give knowledge. The ancient Indian longed to escape from this hard reality, which for him was nothing but illusion, for to him the true was not what his senses perceived, but what lay beyond that. Therefore the first post-Atlantean culture entertained little interest for what occurred externally on the physical plane.

Things were already different among the Persians in the second cultural period, out of which arose Zarathustra, the great pupil of Manu. If we wish to characterize in a few strokes the difference between the Indian and Persian cultures, we may say that a member of the Persian culture felt the physical to be not merely a burden, but a task to be fulfilled. He also looked up into the regions of light, into the spiritual worlds, but he turned his gaze back into the physical world and in his soul he saw how everything divides into the powers of light and the powers of darkness. The physical world became for him a field of work. The Persian said to himself, "There is the beneficent fullness of light, the god Ahura Mazdao or Ormuzd, and there are the dark powers under the leadership of Angramainyush or Ahriman. From Ahura Mazdao comes salvation for men; from Ahriman comes the physical world. We must transform what comes from Ahriman; we must unite with the good gods and vanquish Ahriman, the evil god in matter, by transforming the earth, by becoming beings capable of working upon the earth. By thus vanquishing Ahriman, we make the earth into a medium for the good." The first step toward redeeming the earth was taken by the members of the Persian culture. They hoped that the earth would become a good planet one day, that it would be redeemed,

* For a clear expression of this sentiment, see *Sacred Books and Early Literature of the East* (New York; Parke, Austin, & Lipscomb; 1917), Vol. 9, p. 104.

and that a glorification of Ahura Mazdao, the highest being, would come about.

Thus a man felt who did not gaze up into the sublime heights like the Indian, but planted his feet firmly on this physical earth. A member of the Indian culture, who did not plant his feet in this way, would not have thought thus.

The conquest of the physical plane proceeded further in the third cultural epoch, in the Egyptian-Babylonian-Assyrian-Chaldean culture. At this time, hardly anything remained of the ancient repugnance with which the physical world was felt to be Maya. The Chaldeans looked up to the heavens, and the light of the stars was not merely Maya for them; it was the script that the gods had imprinted on the physical plane. On the paths of the stars the Chaldean priest pursued his way back into the spiritual worlds, and when he was initiated, when he learned to know all the beings who inhabited the planets and the stars, he lifted up his eyes and said, "What I see with my eyes when I gaze up to the heavens is the outer expression of what is given me by occult vision, by initiation. When the initiating priest endows me with the grace of the perception of the divine, then I see God. But all I see externally is not mere illusions; I see in it the handwriting of the gods."

The initiate felt as we would feel if we had been long separated from a friend, then received a letter from him and recognized his familiar handwriting. We see that it was our friend's hand that formed these signs, and we observe the feelings of his heart expressed in them. Approximately thus felt the Chaldean initiate (and also the Egyptian) who was inducted into the holy mysteries and who, while he was in the mystery temple, saw with his spiritual eye the spiritual beings that are connected with our earth. When he went out again, after seeing all this, and cast his eyes on the world of stars, this appeared to him like a letter from the spiritual beings. He perceived a script of the gods. In the blaze of the lightning, in the rolling of the thunder, in the tempest, he saw a revelation of the gods. The gods manifested themselves for him in all that he saw externally. As we feel about the letter from a friend, so did he feel in regard to the outer world. Thus did he feel when he saw the world of the elements, the world of plants, animals, and mountains, the world of the clouds, the world of the stars. Everything was deciphered as a divine script.

The Egyptian had confidence in the laws that man could find in the physical world, through which man can master matter. By this means arose geometry, mathematics. With the help of this, man could rule the elements because he trusted in what his spirit could find, because he believed that he could imprint the spirit upon matter. Thus he could build the pyramids, the temples, and the sphinxes. This was a mighty step in the conquest of the physical plane that was accomplished in the third cultural period. Man had progressed so far that for the first time he was able rightly to respect the physical plane. The physical world began to mean something to him. But what kind of teachers did he require for this?

Man had always needed teachers. Even the initiates had teachers, as in the old Indian time. What kind of teachers did the initiates need? It was necessary that the initiate should be artificially led to see again, during initiation, what man had been able to see previously in his dark clairvoyant consciousness. The neophyte had to be led back into the spiritual world, into the earlier home of the spirit, so that he could communicate to others what he learned from his experiences. For this he needed teachers. The pupils of the Rishis needed teachers who could show them what happened in ancient Lemuria and Atlantis, when man was still clairvoyant. The same was also true of the Persians.

It was different with the Chaldeans, and even more different with the Egyptians. They also had teachers who aided the pupil to develop his powers so that he could see, through clairvoyant vision, into the spiritual world behind the physical world. These were the initiators, who showed what lay behind the physical. But a new teaching, a wholly new method, became necessary in Egypt. In ancient India man had troubled himself little about how what happened in the spiritual world was imprinted upon the physical plane, about the correspondence between gods and men. But in Egypt something else was needed. It was necessary that through initiation the pupil should see the gods, but also that he should see how the gods moved their hands in writing the starry script, how all physical forms had evolved. The ancient Egyptians had schools entirely on the model of those of the Indians, but they also learned how the spiritual forces were correlated with the physical world. Thus they taught new subjects. In ancient India the pupil was shown the spiritual forces through clairvoyance, but in Egypt he was also shown what corresponded physically with the spiritual deeds. He was shown how every member of the physical body corresponded to some spiritual labor, how the heart, for example, corresponded to some spiritual work. The founder of this school, in which was shown not only the spiritual but also its work upon the physical, was the great initiator, *Hermes Trismegistos*. It was he, the thrice-great Thoth, who first showed to men the entire physical world as the handwriting of the gods. Here we see how piece by piece our post-Atlantean cultures embodied their impulses in human evolution. Hermes appeared to the Egyptians like a divine ambassador. He gave then what had to be deciphered as the deed of the gods in the physical world.

In all of this we have somewhat characterized the first three cultural epochs of the post-Atlantean time. Men had learned to value the physical plane.

The fourth epoch, the Greco-Latin, is the period when man came even more into contact with the physical plane. In this time man progressed so far that he not only saw the script of the gods in the physical world, but he also inserted his own self, his spiritual individuality, into the objective world. Such artistic creations as we find in Greece were not known earlier. That man could portray himself in sculpture, creating therein something like his physical self—this was achieved in the fourth cultural period.

In this time we see man's inward spiritual elements step out of him onto the physical plane and flow into matter. This marriage between the spiritual and the material may be seen most clearly in the Greek temple. For everyone who can look back and see this temple, it is a wonderful work. The Greeks had the greatest architectonic gifts. Every art has its climax at some point, and here architecture had its high point. Modeling and painting reached their climax elsewhere. Despite the gigantic pyramids, the most wonderful architecture appears in the Greek temple. For what is attained here? A weak echo may be experienced by one who has an artistic feeling for space, who feels how a horizontal line is related to one that moves in the vertical. A number of cosmic truths light up in the soul that can simply feel how the column carries what is above it. One must be able to feel how all these lines were already invisibly present in space. The Greek artist saw the column as though clairvoyantly, and simply filled what he saw with matter. He saw space as altogether composed of life, as something permeated by living forces.

How can the man of today get some impression of the liveliness that this space-filling had? We see a faint reflection of it in the old painters. For example, we can find paintings where angels float in space, and we have the feeling that the angels support each other. Today little remains of this feeling for space. I shall make no objection to Boecklin's colors,* but all occult space-feeling is missing in him. Such a being as we find above his *Pietá* —you cannot tell if it is supposed to be an angel or some other being—must waken in the observer the feeling that at any minute it may fall on the group below it. This must be emphasized when one tries to explain something of which hardly an inkling can be conveyed today, such as the space-feeling of the Greeks. It must be expressly stated that this was of an occult nature. In a Greek temple it was as if space had given birth to itself out of its own lines. The result of this was that the divine beings for whom the temple was built, and with whom the Greek as a clairvoyant was acquainted, really descended into the temple, really felt comfortable in it. It is true that Pallas Athena, Zeus, etc., were actually within the temples. They had their bodies, their material

* Arnold Boecklin (1827–1901), Swiss painter.

bodies, in these temples. For since these beings could incarnate only as far as an etheric body, they found their dwelling-place in the physical world in these temples. Such a temple could become their physical body, in which their etheric body felt at home.

One who understands the Greek temple knows that it differs profoundly from a Gothic cathedral. This is not a criticism of the Gothic, for the Gothic cathedral is a sublime work of art. But an understanding person can well imagine of a Greek temple, that even if it stood in a solitude with no people anywhere near, even if it were quite alone, it would be a whole. A Greek temple is complete even when nobody is praying in it. It is not soulless, it is not empty, for the god is in it. It is inhabited by the god.

But a Gothic cathedral is only half complete if there are no worshippers within. One who understands this cannot think of a Gothic cathedral standing alone, without a congregation of the faithful, whose thoughts stream into it. All the Gothic forms and ornaments belong to what streams from it. No god, no spiritual being, is close to the Gothic cathedral when the prayers of the faithful are not present. Only when the praying congregation is assembled is the cathedral filled with the divine. This is shown in the very word "Dom," * for this is connected with the "dom" in Christendom and similar words, which signifies something collective. Even the word "Duma" ** is related to this. The Greek temple is not a house for the faithful. It is shaped as a house that the god himself inhabits; it can stand alone. But in the Gothic cathedral one feels at home only when it is filled by the believing throng, when the pious congregation is assembled, when the light of the sun shines through the colored window-panes and the colors are diffused by the fine dust-particles. Then, as often happened, the preacher in the cathedral pulpit would say, "Even as the light is split into many colors, so is the single spiritual light, the divine force, divided among the crowds of souls and split into the diverse forces of the physical plane." Such

* *Dom* is the German word for cathedral.
** The *Duma* was a short-lived parliament in late Czarist Russia.

words were often heard from the preacher. When perception and spiritual experience flowed together in this way, the cathedral was something complete.

As in the great temple buildings, so was it in everything artistic among the Greeks. The marble of their sculptures took on the appearance of life. The Greek expressed in the physical what lived in his spiritual. Among the Greeks the marriage of the spiritual with the physical was a fact.

The Roman went a step further in the conquest of the physical plane. The Greek had the capacity of embodying the soul-spiritual in his works of art, but he still felt himself as part of a whole, of the *polis,* the city-state. He did not yet feel himself as a personality. This was also the case in the earlier cultures. The Egyptian did not feel himself as a separate person, but as an Egyptian, as a member of his people. Thus in Greece we find that a man laid little worth on feeling himself to be a person, but it was his greatest pride to be a Spartan or an Athenian. To be a personality, to be something in the world through the self, was felt for the first time in Rome. That a personality could be something for itself was first true for the Roman. The Romans worked out the concept of the *citizen,* and it was among them that jurisprudence, the science of law, arose. This is correctly regarded as a Roman invention. Only modern jurists, who know nothing of these facts, have had the lack of judgment to assert that law, in this sense, existed earlier. It is nonsense to speak of oriental lawgivers, such as Hammurabi. There were no legal rules earlier; there were only divine commands.* One would have to use harsh words if one were to speak objectively about this kind of science.

The concept of the citizen first became a real feeling in ancient Rome. By that time man had brought the spiritual into the phys-ical world as far as his own individuality. The last Will and Testament was invented in ancient Rome. The will of the single

* Our best modern scholars agree with views here expressed. See Wigmore, *Panorama of the World's Legal Systems* (Washington Law Book Company, 1936).

personality had become so strong that even beyond death it could determine what should be done with its property, its own things. The single personal man was now the determining factor. With this deed man, in his own individuality, had brought the spiritual down to the physical plane. This was the lowest point of evolution.

Man stood at his highest in the Indian culture. At this highest point the Indian still moved in spiritual heights. In the second culture, the ancient Persian, man had already descended a little. In the third culture, the Egyptian, still more. In the fourth culture man descended entirely to the physical plane, into matter. There came a point when man stood at the parting of the ways. Either he could sink lower and lower, or he could achieve the possibility of working up again, of fighting his way back into the spiritual world. But for this a spiritual impulse had to appear on the physical plane, a mighty thrust that could lead man back into the spiritual world. This mighty thrust was given through the appearance of Christ Jesus on earth. The divine-spiritual Christ had to come to men in a physical human body, had to go through a physical appearance in the physical world. Now, when man was wholly in the physical world, the god had to descend to him so he might find the way back into the spiritual world. Previously this would not have been possible.

Today we have followed the evolution of the cultures of the post-Atlantean time down to their lowest point. We have seen how the spiritual impulse occurred through the Christ at the lowest point. Now man must rise again, transfigured by the Christ principle. We shall go on to show how the Egyptian culture emerges again in our time, but permeated by the Christ principle.

LECTURE 10

*Old Myths as Pictures
of Cosmic Facts.
Darkening of Man's
Spiritual Consciousness.
The Initiation Principle
of the Mysteries.*

September 12, 1908

THERE are many myths and sagas of the ancient Egyptians that were well-known to the spiritual-scientific world conception and are again becoming known, but are not transmitted by the external historical traditions touching on the Egyptians. Some of these myths were preserved for us in the form in which they became domesticated in Greece, for most of the Greek legends that do not relate to Zeus and his family, stem from the Egyptian mysteries. We shall occupy ourselves today with all sorts of mythical things that we can put to good use, despite the assertion of modern cultural history that Greek mythology contains little of value.

Why should we examine this other side of human evolution, the spiritual side? All that we see on the physical plane always remains an event and fact of the physical plane. But in the science of the spirit, we are interested not only in what lives on the physical plane, but also in all that occurs in the spiritual worlds.

From what we have heard in our lectures we know what happens to man between death and a new birth. We need only recall that in death man enters the condition of consciousness that we call kamaloka, in which, although he has become a spiritual being, he is held fast by the astral body. This is the time when man still demands something from the physical world, when he suffers from the fact that he is no longer in the physical world. Then comes the time when he must prepare himself for a new life, the consciousness-condition of devachan, where he is no longer immediately connected with the physical world and with physical impressions.

In order to understand how life in kamaloka differs from life in devachan, let us consider two examples. We know that as soon as he has died, man does not lose his cravings and desires. Let us assume that during his life a person was a gourmet, taking great pleasure in choice food. When he dies, he does not at once lose this desire for enjoyment, this craving for dainties. These wishes do not live in the physical body, but in the astral. Therefore, since man retains his astral body after death, he also retains the craving, but he lacks the organ with which to satisfy this craving, the physical body. The craving for food depends on the astral body rather than on the physical, and after death the person feels a real lust for what pleased him most in life. For this reason he suffers after death until he has weaned himself of the desire for enjoyment, until he has sloughed off all the cravings that he had cultivated through the physical organs. Throughout this period he remains in kamaloka. Then begins the time when he no longer makes demands of the type that can be satisfied only through physical organs. Then he enters into devachan.

In the same proportion that man ceases to be fettered to the physical world he begins to develop a consciousness for the devachanic world. This world becomes more and more illuminated, but he does not yet have an ego-consciousness there, such as he had in this life. He is not yet independent there. In the devachanic life he feels like a limb, like an organ, of the entire spiritual world. As the hand, if it could feel, would feel itself to be a

105

member of the physical organism, so man feels in his devachanic consciousness that he is a limb of the spiritual world, a limb of the higher beings. He must grow toward his independence. But he already cooperates in the cosmos; he works on the plant kingdom from out the spiritual world. Man cooperates in all this, not for his own account, but as a ministering member of the spiritual world.

When we thus describe what man experiences between death and a new birth, we must not imagine that the events of the devachanic world are not also subject to change. People are apt to believe privily that, although our earth is changeable, everything up yonder, beyond death, remains the same. This is by no means the case. When we describe the sojourn in devachan in this way, this means only that this is approximately the way things are there at the present time. But let us remember how it was when our souls were incarnated during the Egyptian culture. Then we looked upon the gigantic pyramids and the other mighty buildings. In earlier times things looked very different on this side, on the physical side. The countenance of the earth has changed greatly since then. We need only look into materialistic science and we shall find, for example, how a few thousand years ago there were entirely different animals in Europe, how Europe looked quite different. The face of the earth is constantly changing, whence it comes that man is always entering into new conditions of existence. This is obvious to everyone. But when we describe the conditions of the spiritual world, people are prone to believe that what happened there when they died a thousand years before Christ, is exactly the same as what happens when they are reborn and die again today. Just as the physical plane changes, so do things change in the other world. When man entered into devachan from an Egyptian or a Greek life, his sojourn there was something quite different from what it is today. Evolution occurs there also. It is only natural that we should describe the present conditions in devachan, but these have changed. This could have been surmised from what was brought before us in the last lecture.

106

We have seen how, when we go back to the Atlantean time, man lived more in the spiritual world, how he moved about in the spiritual world during sleep. We found that this decreases steadily after that time. But if we go back far enough we find that man once lived entirely in the spiritual world. In ancient times the difference between sleep and death was not great. In primeval antiquity man had long periods of sleep, approximately as long as the time now consumed by an incarnation and the life after death. Through the fact that man descended to the physical plane, he became ever more entangled in this physical plane. We have shown how the Indian gazed into a high world and how, in Persia, man already attempted to conquer the physical plane. Man descended ever further, and in the Greco-Latin time there occurred a marriage between spirit and matter, between the spiritual worlds and the physical plane. The more man approached the middle of this last epoch, the more he learned to love the physical world and take an interest in it. As this occurred, everything that we call experiences between death and a new birth also changed.

If we go back to the first part of the post-Atlantean period, we find that men took little interest in the physical world. The initiates of that time could withdraw into lofty worlds, into the devachanic worlds, and they communicated their experiences to the others. In the man who, with all his thoughts and all his senses, felt himself withdrawn into the true world, into his real home, the effect was that he took little interest in the conditions of the physical plane. But when he rose into devachan, after having barely connected himself with the physical world, he possessed in devachan a comparatively clear consciousness. When such a man incarnated again in the Persian culture, he felt himself more connected with physical matter, and he lost some of the clarity of his consciousness in devachan. In the Egypto-Chaldean time, when man began to feel some affection for the external physical world, his consciousness in devachan already became clouded and shadowy. This consciousness was still of a nature higher than that of his consciousness in the physical world, but it declined steadily in degree and became ever darker up to the Greco-Latin time. During all this time the devachanic consciousness became ever darker and more shadowy. It was not a dream consciousness; this was never the case. It was a consciousness of which man was fully aware. In the course of evolution it became darkened.

The mysteries existed principally in order to enable man again to illuminate his consciousness, rather than have only a shadowy consciousness in the spiritual world. Let us reflect that if there had been no mysteries there would have been no initiates, in which case man would have had an increasingly vague and shadowy consciousness in the spiritual worlds. Only through the fact that, parallel with the darkening of devachanic consciousness, initiation into the mysteries continued, together with the acquisition of certain faculties with which selected persons could look into the spiritual worlds in full clarity—only through the fact that the initiates could speak of this in myths and sagas, was it possible for a ray of light to penetrate into the devachanic consciousness between death and a new birth. But all those who had made themselves comfortable in the physical world experienced this fading away of consciousness in the spiritual world. It was no fairy tale but plain truth, that the initiates in the Eleusinian mysteries were able to have a special experience. The principle of initiation is that, even during his life, man can ascend to the spiritual worlds and learn what takes place there. The initiate of that time was actually able to learn directly from the shades in the spiritual world. The following is really the statement of an initiate: "Better a beggar on earth than a king in the realm of shades." * This statement is made out of the initiates' experience. We cannot take such things deeply enough, and we only understand them when we know the facts of the spiritual world.

Now let us bring into more concrete form what we touched upon abstractly yesterday.

Had nothing occurred other than man's descent into the phys-

* These are the words of Achilles in Book XI of the *Odyssey*.

ical world, consciousness between death and a new birth would have grown ever darker. Ultimately men would have entirely lost their connection with the spiritual world. Now, however singular it may appear to those who are only slightly infected with some form of materialism, what I am about to say is true. Had nothing else intervened in human evolution, mankind would have succumbed to spiritual death. But there is a possibility of illuminating the consciousness between death and a new birth, and this illumination can be achieved either through initiation or (to a lower degree) through man's participating in the spiritual world during this life, having experiences that do not die out with his bodies, but remain connected with the eternal core of his being, even in the spiritual world. This was the concern of the mysteries and of all spiritual development. It was the concern of the great initiates before Christ and, above all, of the Being whom we call Christ. All other initiates were in a certain sense forerunners of the Christ; they were harbingers who pointed to the coming of the Christ.

The advent of the Christ-figure will now be described. Let us imagine a man who has never heard anything of the Christ, who has never been able to absorb the mysteries of the Gospel of John, who has never been able to say, "I will imitate the life and work of the Christ; I will try to take his percepts into my own being." If we add that the Christ had never approached this man, he would not be able to take with him into the spiritual world the treasure that the man of today must take with him if he is to avoid the darkening of his consciousness. What man takes with him as a picture of Christ is a force that brightens the consciousness after death, that saves man from the fate that all men would have had if Christ had not appeared. If Christ had not appeared, the human essence would have been maintained, but the consciousness after death could not have been illuminated. This is what gives real meaning to the advent of the Christ, that something was embodied into the core of man's being that has a wide significance. The event of Golgotha preserves man from spiritual death if he makes it one with his own being.

We should not think that the other great leaders of mankind did not have a similar significance. There is no question of claiming some exclusive dogma for Christianity. That would be an offence against true Christianity, for anyone acquainted with the facts knows that Christianity was also taught in the ancient mysteries. Such words as those of Augustine are profoundly true: "What is called the Christian religion today existed already among the ancients and was present with the beginnings of the human race. But when Christ appeared in the flesh the true religion, which was already in existence, received the name of Christian." What is important is not the name, but that we rightly understand the significance of the Christ impulse. Christ was the figure that appeared at the lowest point in evolution, but Buddha, Hermes, and the other great beings were in complete possession of the prophetic consciousness that the Christ would come, that he lived in them.

We can see this clearly when we study the figure of Buddha, and we must be quite clear as to what he was. What was Buddha, in reality? Here we must touch on something that can be said only among students of the science of the spirit. It is customary for people, even for theosophists, to conceive the mysteries of reincarnation in much too simple a way. One should not imagine that a soul that is embodied today in its three sheaths was embodied in the same way in a foregoing incarnation, and again in one before that, always according to the same scheme. The secrets are much more complicated. Although H. P. Blavatsky took great pains to show her intimate pupils how complicated these secrets were, the matter is still not rightly understood today. People think simply that a soul goes into a body ever and again. But it is not so simple. Often we cannot fit a historical figure into such a scheme if we wish to understand it correctly. We must go about the matter in a much more complicated way.

Already in Atlantis we meet beings who were among men as our fellows are today, but whom man saw and learned to know when he was in the spiritual world, severed from the body. We have already pointed out how man learned to know Thor,

Zeus, Wotan, Baldur as actual companions. By day he lived in the physical world, but in the other condition of consciousness he learned to know spiritual beings who were going through a stage of evolution different from his. In this primeval period of the earth man did not yet have so solid a body as today; there was as yet nothing like a bony skeleton. The Atlantean body could be seen with physical eyes only to a certain extent. But there were beings who descended only so far as to incarnate in an etheric body. Then there were beings who still embodied themselves at that time, when the air was permeated by water-vapors. When man still lived in the water-fog atmosphere, these incarnations were possible for them. Such a figure was the later Wotan, for example. He said to himself, "If man incarnates in this fluid matter, then I can also." Such a being assumed a human form and moved about in the physical world. But as the earth condensed and man took on ever denser forms, Wotan said, "No, I shall not go into this dense matter." Then he remained in invisible worlds, in worlds removed from the earth.

This was the general case with the divine spiritual beings. But from then on, they could do something else. They could enter into a sort of connection with men who approached them, who evolved upward from below. We may imagine it thus. Man's evolutionary course was such that he was approaching his lowest point of development. Up to this point the gods had proceeded in company with men. Now they took another path, which was invisible for men on the physical plane. But men who lived according to the directions of the initiates, thereby purifying their finer bodies, approached them in a certain way. A man who was incarnated in the flesh, if he purified himself, could do this in such a way that he could be overshadowed by such a being, who could not descend as far as the physical body. The physical body would have been too coarse for such a being. The result for such a man was that the astral and etheric bodies were permeated by a higher being, which had no other human form for itself but could enter into another being and proclaim itself through this other being.

111

When we are familiar with this phenomenon, we shall not regard incarnation as such a simple matter. There can perfectly well be a person who is the reincarnation of an earlier man, who has developed himself so far and purified his three bodies to such an extent that he is now a vessel for a higher being. Buddha became such a vessel for Wotan. The same being who was called Wotan in the Germanic myths, appeared again as Buddha. Buddha and Wotan are even related linguistically.

So we can say that much of what was in the mysteries of the Atlantean time continued in what the Buddha was able to announce. This is in harmony with the fact that what the Buddha experienced is something that the gods had experienced in those spiritual spheres, and that men also had experienced when they were still in those spheres. As the teaching of Wotan thus appeared again, it was a doctrine that paid little attention to the physical plane, emphasizing that the physical plane is a place of woe, and that redemption from it is important. Much of the Wotan-being spoke in the Buddha. Hence it is that stragglers from Atlantis have shown the deepest understanding for the Buddha-teaching. Among the Asiatic population there are races that have remained at the Atlantean level, although externally they must, of course, move ahead with the earth evolution. Among the Mongolian peoples much of Atlantis has remained. They are stragglers from the old population of Atlantis. The stationary character in the Mongolian population is a heritage from Atlantis. Therefore the teachings of the Buddha are especially serviceable to such peoples, and Buddhism has made great strides among them.

The world moves onward, following its course. One who can look deeply into the evolution of the world does not make choices, does not say that he has more inclination for this or that. He says that what religion a people has is a spiritual necessity. The European population, because it has ensnared itself in the physical world, finds it impossible to feel its way into Buddhism, to identify itself with the innermost teachings of the Buddha. Buddhism could never become a religion for all of humanity.

For him who can see, there is no sympathy or antipathy here, but only a judgment in accordance with the facts. It would be an error to wish to spread Christianity from a center in Asia, where other peoples are still settled, and Buddhism would be equally false for the European population. No religious view is right if it is not suited to the innermost needs of the time, and such a view will never be able to give a cultural impulse. These are things that we must grasp if we want to understand all the real connections.

But one should not believe that the historical appearance of the Buddha immediately reveals all that lies within it. If I were to expound all this, I would need several hours. As yet we are far from having unraveled the complications of the historical Buddha. Something still lived in the Buddha. This is not only a being who came over out of the Atlantean time and incarnated in him who incidentally was also a human Buddha. In addition to this something else was contained in him, something of which he could say, "I cannot yet comprehend this. It is something that ensouls me, but I only participate in it." This is the Christ-being. This had already ensouled the great prophets. It was a well-known being in the more ancient mysteries, and everywhere and always men had pointed to him who was to come.

And he came! But again he came in such a way that he accommodated himself to the historical necessities that lie behind evolution. Without special preparation he could not incarnate himself in a physical body. It was still possible for him to incarnate in a sort of subconsciousness in the Buddha. But he could incarnate to live on the earth only if a physical body, and etheric body, and an astral body were specially prepared for him. The Christ had the greatest powers, but he could incarnate only if, through another being, a physical, an etheric, and an astral body had been completely cleansed and purified. Thus the incarnation of the Christ could occur only if another being appeared who had developed himself to this point. This was Jesus of Nazareth. He had proceeded so far in his evolution that he was able, during his life, to purify his physical, etheric, and astral bodies in such a way that it was possible for him, in the thirtieth year of his life, to abandon these bodies, yet to leave them capable of life, usable for a higher being.

Often, when I have stated that a high stage of development was necessary for Jesus to be able to sacrifice his bodies, people have made a strange objection: "But that is not a sacrifice; nothing could be more beautiful! One cannot speak of a sacrifice when it is a question of turning over his bodies to such a high Being!" Yes, it is beautiful, and the sacrifice is not great when one looks at it abstractly; but only try to do the deed. Everyone would like to make the sacrifice, but only let them try it. One must have extraordinary forces if one is to purify the bodies in such a way as to leave them while they are capable of life, and to attain these forces, many sacrifices are necessary. To be able to do this, Jesus of Nazareth had to be an extraordinarily high individuality. The Gospel of John indicates where Jesus abandoned his physical, etheric, and astral bodies and entered into the spiritual world, and where the Christ-being entered into the threefold corporeality. This happened at the baptism of Jesus in the Jordan. At this moment something significant occurred in the corporeality of Jesus of Nazareth. For the materialistic mind, what I now say is bound to be an abomination. Something special occurred in the physical body of Jesus of Nazareth. If we wish to understand what occurred at the moment of the baptism, when the Christ entered into Jesus, we must turn our attention to something that will appear singular, but is nevertheless true.

In the course of human evolution, the various organs have developed bit by bit, gradually working out their form. We have seen how, when the organs had reached the level of the hips, certain structures and functions appeared in man. Then, too, as the human individuality became more self-reliant, a hardening of the bony system set in. The more independent man became, the more his bony system hardened and the greater became the power of death. We must bear this in mind if we are to understand the following in the right way. Whence comes it that man must die and the body must completely disintegrate? It comes

114

from the fact that in the human body something can be burned, even down to the bones. Fire has power over the human bone-substance. Man has no power, at least no conscious power, over his bones. This power still lies outside man's abilities. In the moment when, at the baptism in Jordan, the Christ drew into the body of Jesus of Nazareth, in that moment the bony system of this being became something entirely different from what it is in other men. This was something that had never happened before and has not happened again to this day. With the Christ-being there entered into the Jesus-being something that had power over the forces that burn up the bones. Today the building up of the bones has not yet been placed within man's discretion. But this power reached right down into the bones. The conscious power of the Christ-being extended into the bones. This is part of the meaning of the baptism by John. Therewith something was implanted in the earth that can be called the supremacy over death, for death first appeared in the world with the bones. Through the fact that power over the bones entered the human body, the victory over death also came into the world. Here a deep mystery is expressed. Something in the highest degree holy entered into the bony system of Jesus of Nazareth through the Christ. Therefore it was not to be touched. For this reason the scripture had to be fulfilled: "A bone of him shall not be broken." * That would have allowed human power to meddle in divine forces. Here we are gazing into a deep mystery of human evolution.

Here we come to a significant concept of esoteric Christianity, which can show us how this Christianity is permeated with the highest truths. We come to the remainder of what confronts us in the baptism. Through the fact that the Christ-being took possession of the three bodies in which the ego-being of Jesus formerly abode, a Being was bound up with the earth that had earlier had its dwelling-place on the sun. It had formerly been bound up with the earth until the moment when the sun departed from the earth. At that time the Christ also departed, and from then on

* The reference is to the Gospel of John, XIX:36.

he could exercise his power upon the earth only from outside. In the moment of the baptism, the high Christ-spirit again united himself in the full sense with the earth. Formerly he worked from outside, overshadowing the prophets and working in the mysteries. Now he was actually incarnated in a physical human body on the earth. If a being had been able to look down for thousands of years from a remote point in the universe, such a being as could see not only the physical earth but also its spiritual streams, its astral and etheric bodies, it would have seen significant events in the moment of the baptism by John, and in the moment when the blood flowed from Christ's wounds on Golgotha. The earth's astral body was profoundly changed thereby. At this moment it took up something different; it took on different colors. A new force was implanted in the earth. What earlier had worked from without, again became united with the earth, and thereby the attractive power between sun and earth will grow so strong that sun and earth will again unite, and man will unite with the sun-spirits. It was the Christ who gave the possibility that the earth can again unite with the sun and be in the bosom of the Godhead.

This is the event that occurred, and its meaning. We had to expound this in order to understand what entered into the earth with the Christ. Through this we can grasp how, through union with the Christ, man can absorb something by which his consciousness will again be illuminated after death. If we keep this in mind we shall also be able to grasp how there is evolution for the period between death and a new birth. Now let us ask for whose sake all this took place.

At first, man lived in the bosom of the Godhead. Then he descended to the physical plane. Had he remained above, he would never have achieved his present consciousness of self. He would never have received an ego. Only in the physical body could he kindle the consciousness of self in its bright clarity. He had to encounter external objects and become able to distinguish himself from the objects; he had to descend into the physical world. Only for the sake of man's ego did it happen that man descended. In respect to his ego man stems from the gods. This ego descended out of the spiritual world; it was forged on the physical body so that it might become bright and clear. It is precisely the hardened matter of the human body that has given man his self-conscious ego, that has made it possible for him to attain knowledge. But it also chained him to the earth-mass, to the rock-mass.

Before he achieved his ego, man had physical body, etheric body, and astral body. As the ego gradually evolved in these three bodies, it transformed them. We must be quite clear that all man's higher members work on the physical body. The physical body is as it is because the etheric, astral, and ego work on it. In a certain way all the organs of the physical body are as they are because the higher members have also been altered. Through the domination of the astral body, the backward beings became the different animal forms—the birds, for example. Through the fact that the ego became ever more conscious of itself, it also altered the astral body. We have already said that men separated themselves into groups. What we call the apocalyptic beasts are types, in which this or that higher member has the upper hand. The ego gained predominance in the manform. All the organs are adapted to man's higher members. When the ego entered into the astral body and wholly permeated it, certain organs took form in man and in the animals that branched off later. Thus, for example, a particular organ may stem from the fact that an ego made its entry upon the earth. On the moon, no ego was connected with the beings in human evolution. Certain organs are connected with this development: the gall and the liver. The gall is the physical expression of the astral body. It is not bound up with the ego, but the ego works on the astral body, and from this the forces work on the gall.

Now let us draw together the entire picture that the initiate made so clear to the Egyptian. The self-conscious man has been shackled to the earth-body. Imagine the man fettered to the earth-rock, fettered to the physical body—and in the course of evolution something arises that gnaws at his immortality. Think of the functions that have called forth the liver. They have arisen through the fact that the body was chained to the rocks of earth. The astral body gnaws at it.

This is the picture that was given to the pupil in Egypt and made its way into Greece as the saga of Prometheus. We must not lay rough hands upon such a myth. We must not rob the butterfly of the dust on its wings. We must leave the dust on its wings. We must leave the dew on the blossoms instead of twisting and torturing such pictures. We should not say that Prometheus means this or that. We should try to present the real occult facts, and then try to understand the pictures that have arisen out of the occult facts and have passed over into the consciousness of man.

The Egyptian initiate led his pupil up to the point where he could grasp man's ego-development. Such a picture was intended to shape his spirit. But the pupil was not to seize the facts with heavy hands. The picture was to stand bright and livingly before him, and the initiate did not wish to press dry banal concepts into the truths he could give. He wanted to present truth in pictures. Poetry has done much for the Prometheus saga, beautifying and ornamenting it. We should add nothing to the occult facts, but leave this delicate embellishment to the artist.

We must still point to something else. Man, when he arrived on earth, was not yet endowed with the ego. Before the ego was secreted into the astral body, other forces had possession of this body. Then the light-flowing astral body was permeated by the ego. Before the ego entered therein, the astral forces of divine-spiritual beings had been sent into man from outside. The astral body was also present, but illuminated by divine-spiritual beings. The astral body was pure and bright, and it flowed around what was present as the rudiments of the physical and etheric bodies. It flowed around and through these, and was quite pure. But egoism entered with the advent of the ego, and the astral body was darkened and lost its golden flow. This was lost more and more, until man had descended to the lowest point of the physical plane in the Greco-Latin time.

Then men had to consider how they could win back the pure flow of the astral body, and there arose in the Eleusinian mysteries what was known as the search for the original purity of the astral body. One aim of the Eleusinian mysteries, and also of the Egyptians, was to recapture the astral body in its pristine golden flow. The quest for the Golden Fleece was one of the probations of the Egyptian initiations, and this has been preserved for us in the wonderful saga of the voyage of Jason and the Argonauts. We have seen the development. When the form of the lower organs still resembled the boats of which we have spoken, the astral body in the water-earth still had a golden sheen. In the water-earth, man's astral body was permeated with golden light. The search for the astral body is portrayed in the voyage of the Argonauts. In a refined and subtle way we must bring the quest for the Golden Fleece into connection with the Egyptian myth.

External historical facts are linked with spiritual facts. One should not believe that this is mere symbol. The voyage of the Argonauts actually took place, just as the Trojan War actually took place. Outer events are the physiognomy for inner events; all these are historical events. For the Greek neophyte the historical fact took place anew inwardly: the journey after the Golden Fleece, the achieving of the pure astral body.

This is what we wanted to bring before our souls today. On this basis we shall become acquainted with other things from the mysteries, and then we shall find how the Egyptian mysteries are connected with the life of today.

LECTURE 11

The Ancient Egyptian Doctrine
of Evolution.
The Cosmic View of the Organs
and their Coarsening in Modern Times.

September 13, 1908

A T various points in this cycle of lectures we have tried to
present the facts of post-Atlantean evolution, and we have
indicated that in our time there is a kind of repetition or resurrection of the experiences that mankind went through during the
Egypto-Chaldean culture. It has been stated that the Indian period will repeat itself in the seventh period, the Persian in the
sixth, the Egyptian in our time, and that the fourth, the Greco-
Latin, stands by itself, so to say. Now, connecting the Egyptian
time and our own, we shall try to indicate how a certain recrudescence of outer and inner experiences is to be seen when we
bring our time into connection with the Egyptian.

We have seen that in the spiritual worlds there exist mysterious
forces, to which there correspond certain other forces in the
physical world which effectuate the appearance of these repetitions. Thus do these resurrections of outer and inner experiences
originate. In the middle between these stands the Greco-Latin
period, during which the Christ appeared upon the earth and the

Mystery of Golgotha took place. It was also pointed out that not only the external evolutionary relationships on the physical plane had changed, but that also the relationships in the spiritual world had become different. I have described how the soul was in the Egyptian time, when it looked upon the gigantic pyramids, how different it was when it reincarnated in the Greco-Latin period, and how different it is in our time. We have seen that not only does this occur, but that also for the period between death and a new birth, in kamaloka and devachan, there takes place a sort of progress or transformation, so that the soul does not experience the same thing when it enters into kamaloka or devachan from an Egyptian, a Greek, or a modern body. Externally the world of the physical plane alters, but progress also occurs in the spiritual world so that the soul always experiences something different there.

It is primarily from the standpoint of this "beyond" that today we shall consider the mighty event of the Christ's appearance on our earth. We shall approach in a much deeper way the question, What significance has the advent of the Christ on our earth? What significance has the Christ's appearance for the dead souls, for the life on the other side, the spiritual side, of existence? For this purpose we must explore many different things that affected souls in the Egyptian period both within and beyond the physical plane.

From our studies of the earlier great epochs of earth evolution we can derive that the Egypto-Chaldean period furnishes a mirroring in knowledge and experience of what happened in the Lemurian time, of what happened on the earth during and after the departure of the moon. What men experienced then, they experienced again as a memory in what the Egyptian initiates gave them. The Egyptian initiate himself experienced during his initiation events that man otherwise experiences only when he passes through the portal of death. To be sure, the Egyptian initiate experienced this in a different way than does the ordinary person who dies. He experienced it differently and in a much fuller way. It will be well for us now, as a basis for these considerations, to describe the essence of Egyptian initiation in a few words. This initiation is essentially different from that of the time after Christ, for through his advent initiation was fundamentally altered.

We have seen that men had to descend further and further into the material world, gaining increasing interest in the physical world. In the same proportion, however, the experience in the spiritual world between death and a new birth became more pale and shadowy. The livelier man's consciousness became in the physical world, the more he enjoyed being there, the more he discovered the laws of the physical plane, the dimmer his consciousness in the spiritual world became. The consciousness in the spiritual world reached its low point in the Greco-Latin time. But even before man had fully descended into these depths of matter, it had become impossible for him, within the physical body, to experience completely what one must experience if, during the period between birth and death, one seeks to gain insight into the spiritual world.

The initiation event may be briefly described, and it is the same for initiations before and after Christ, although the conclusion is different. Initiation is nothing other than man's gaining the capacity of developing organs of vision in his higher bodies. Today man sees darkness when it is night; he is in the dark. This is because man has no organs of perception in his astral body. As the eyes and ears have formed themselves into physical organs of perception, so supersensible organs must be developed out of the higher members and assimilated into them. This occurs through certain exercises of concentration and meditation being given to the pupil. These exercises are performed after the pupil has first surveyed the knowledge of the spiritual worlds that can be given by the initiates. It has always been the case that the pupils had to learn what we today would call elementary theosophy. Much more strongly than today it was required that the pupils become acquainted with the truth in a regular progression. When there was enough theoretical preparation, and when the pupils were sufficiently mature, the exercises were given to them. These exercises have a definite purpose.

When in his daily life man lets the impressions of the senses work upon him, these impressions bring certain fruits for the ordinary life on the physical plane. These impressions pass over into the astral body, which in turn transmits them to the ego. But these impressions are such that man cannot hold them fast when, with his astral body and ego, he slips out of his physical and etheric bodies during the night. What man receives in this way from the physical plane does not penetrate into him so strongly that he can retain it as a permanent impression. But when a person performs the exercises of meditation and concentration, these are so adjusted, in accordance with thousands of years of experience, that the astral body no longer loses the impressions, but retains them when it slips out of the physical body in the night. Through the exercises the astral body receives plastic impressions, which shape and member it as the physical organs have been membered. Thus the astral body is worked on for certain periods through these exercises. Thereby the supersensible organs of vision are imprinted on the astral body. It would be a long time, however, before man could use his organs of vision if they were imprinted only into his astral body. Something further must take place so that the astral body, when it returns into the etheric body, may stamp upon that body, like the impression of a seal, what has taken shape within itself. Only when what has taken shape in the astral body imprints itself upon the etheric body, only then does the illumination take place that makes it possible for the person to see the spiritual world as he sees the physical world today.

Here we can begin to grasp what kind of an impulse we have received through the appearance of Christ on earth. In the old initiations the astral body had the strength to work upon the etheric body only when the etheric body had been lifted out of the physical body. This was because at that time the etheric body, had it remained connected with the physical body, would have exerted so much resistance that it could not have received the imprint of what the astral body had formed within itself. In the ancient initiations, therefore, for a period of three and a half days, the candidate was put into a deathlike condition in which the physical body was deserted by the etheric body while this latter, freed from the physical, united itself with the astral body.

The astral then stamped into the etheric all that had been built into the astral through the exercises. When the hierophant again awakened the candidate, the latter was illuminated. He knew what took place in the spiritual world, for he had made a remarkable journey during the three and a half days. He had been led through the fields of the spiritual world. He had seen what went on there, and he knew from direct experience what another person could learn only through revelation. A person thus initiated could, out of his own experiences, give knowledge of the beings who were in the spiritual world, beyond the physical plane.

When man had not yet descended so far into the physical plane, he could learn what was experienced in the spiritual world. There the candidate became acquainted with the true form of Osiris, Isis, and Horus. The initiate saw the contents of the myths during this journey into the spiritual world. He could then transmit this to other persons when he had dressed it as myth or saga. He saw all this; he saw in what a special way the Osiris influences had shaped themselves when the moon had withdrawn from the earth; he saw how Horus issued from Isis and Osiris; he saw the four human types, the bull, the lion, the eagle, and the true man. He also saw what happened to man between death and a new birth. The Sphinx appeared to him as a real form; he experienced it. He could say, "Oh, I have seen the Sphinx, man as he was when he still had an animal-like form, and his etheric body—similar to the human—only projected out of this animal-like form!" The Sphinx was a real experience for the initiate. He even heard the question of the Sphinx with its enigmatic content. He saw how the human body prepared itself out of the animality, at a time when the head was only an etheric form, the ether-head of the Sphinx. This was truth for the initiate, as were also the older forms of the gods, who had, so to speak, taken a different course of evolution.

It has recently been said that certain beings pursued a different path in evolution. The individuality of Wotan, for example, takes such a different course. Up to a certain stage it travels together with man, but then it does not descend so deeply. Man descends further into matter and only later will he again join these beings, who are completing their evolution in the earth-time. We have seen that a time came when Wotan no longer walked on our earth. Such beings, however, were not like Osiris and Isis. These latter were beings who had branched off still earlier, who completed their evolution on a higher level in full invisibility. These forms went through their special experiences.

Let us look back into the Lemurian period. At that time the etheric was not yet manlike in its form. In his etheric body man was still similar to the animals, and the gods who descended then had to accommodate themselves to the same animal forms in which man lived on the earth. If a being wishes to enter into a certain plane, it must fulfill the conditions of that plane. This is also the case here. The divine beings who were connected with the earth during the departure of the sun and moon, who were on the earth, had to take on a form that was possible at that time, an animal-like form. And since the Egyptian religious views present in a certain way a recapitulation of the Lemurian time, the Egyptian initiate looked upon the gods, Osiris and Isis for example, as having animal-like forms. He still saw the higher gods with animal heads. Therefore from an occult view it was quite correct when such forms were represented with the head of a hawk or a ram in accordance with what the initiates knew. The gods were portrayed in the forms they had when they walked the earth. The outer images could only resemble what the initiate saw, but they were faithfully reproduced. The various divine beings changed a good deal. The forms in Lemuria were different from those in Atlantis. In those times beings went through much more rapid changes than they do now. In addition, these forms were still filled with spirit. When one looks back on them one sees them in their three bodies, but illuminated and rayed through by the astral and etheric light. This was accurately por-trayed in the pictures. Modern men may laugh over the forms that were represented, but they do not know how realistic they were.*

* Fantastic speculation on the reason why the Egyptians worshipped

There was one being who performed special services in that period of human evolution when, through the cosmic-tellurian powers, the combining intellect was being organized in man. At that time the physical brain was prepared in such a way that man was able to develop intelligence later. This capacity was implanted in man and reckoned as one of the deeds of the god Manu. What was worked into man as intelligence was connected with this. If today we examine a person in whom a well-formed ability for judging and combining is present, if we examine him clairvoyantly, we find a strong expression and reflection of this fact in a green glittering and shining of the astral body, of the astral aura. The capacity for combining shows itself in green colors in the aura, especially in those who have keen mathematical understanding. The ancient Egyptian initiates saw the god who implanted the faculty of intelligence in men, and in portraying him they painted him green* because they saw the green shimmering of his luminous astral and etheric form. Today this is still the color that glitters in the aura when the person's intelligence is stirred. Much time could be devoted to these connections if people really wanted to study this wonderful realism of the forms of the Egyptian gods. These representations of the divine forms, through the fact that they were so realistic and not at all arbitrary, had magical power; and one who could see more deeply would perceive that many mysteries were present in the coloring of these ancient forms. Here one can see deep into the workings of human evolution.

We have seen how what the initiates saw was retained in the Sphinx. Of course, this was not retained in a photographic way, yet it was realistic. But the forms were always changing. The form of the Sphinx gives an image of how man once looked. His present form has been shaped by man himself. We know that through evolution on the earth various animal forms have been

animal-headed gods began in classical times. See Plutarch, *On Isis and Osiris,* Sec. 72.

  * For pictures of the Green Osiris see the frontispieces in both volumes of Budge, *Osiris and the Egyptian Resurrection,* and in Volumes II, X and XII of Maspero and Rappaport, *History of Egypt* (London, Grolier, 1901). See also text in Budge, Vol. II, p. 355.

split off. What is an animal form? It is a form that has remained static, while man proceeded further in evolution. In these forms we see arrested stages of evolution, to the extent that these forms have become physical. In the spiritual something else has taken place. What man is spiritually has nothing to do with his physical forebears. Only the physical is connected with that. Man does not descend from the animals; the animal forms have remained unchanged. In man, however, the shape has been transformed to a certain level. The animals are previous physical human forms fallen into decadence. The situation is different in another realm of evolution. Not only have the physical forms of the animals remained unchanged, but also the rudiments of the etheric and astral forms as well. Just as the lion, at the time when it split off, looked quite different than now, so certain soul-spiritual forms degenerate in the course of time when they remain at a particular stage. It is a law of the spiritual world that anything that stands still on the same level of spirit or soul becomes more and more decadent.

If, for example, the Sphinx stands still, it degenerates and receives a form that is like a caricature of what it originally was. The Sphinx has been preserved in this way on the astral plane up to our own time. To those who, as initiates or in some other lawful manner, penetrate into the higher worlds, these decadent forms have little interest, being only decayed vagabonds in the spiritual world. But when, in exceptional cases, persons equipped with inferior clairvoyant gifts are led into the astral world, such decadent forms approach them. The true Sphinx approached Oedipus, but it has not died even yet. Up to today it has not died; it only approaches man in another form. When persons who have remained standing at a certain stage of evolution, among the peasants perhaps, rest in the fields at midday in the hot glow of the summer sun, and fall asleep, they may have what could be called a latent sun-stroke. Through such an impact on the physical body, the astral and etheric are loosened from a part of the physical. Then such persons are translated to the astral plane and they see this last decadent offspring of the Sphinx. This apparition is called by different names. In certain regions it is called the midday woman. Many people in the country will recount that they have met the midday woman. She appears in many regions under many different names. She is a descendent of the ancient Sphinx, and as the ancient Sphinx put questions to the men who experienced her, so this midday woman also asks questions. You may hear it told how the midday woman asks endless questions of the men whom she meets. This torment by questions is a relic of the old Sphinx. The midday woman has grown out of the ancient Sphinx. This indicates how evolution proceeds beyond the physical world, how whole tribes of spiritual beings decline until at last they are mere shadows of what they were originally. Here we see another characteristic of the way in which things are connected in evolution. We have mentioned this so it may be seen how manifold evolution is.

Now, to understand everything correctly, we must give some thought to the fact that in the course of time man has organized the fourth member, the ego, into what he brought with him at the beginning of earth evolution as his physical, etheric, and astral bodies. I have shown how this ego permeates the astral body, claims it for itself so that it dominates it as higher spiritual beings formerly dominated it. It is a deed of the higher beings that this ego was implanted in the astral body. If evolution had proceeded further in accordance with the views of certain higher beings, it would have been a different evolution from what has actually taken place. However, certain beings remained unchanged. They had not become capable of collaborating in implanting the ego in the astral body.

When man appeared on the earth he consisted of the physical, etheric, and astral bodies, all of which he shaped further. Now he was endowed with egohood by certain sublime beings who had their dwellings mainly on the sun and moon. These beings collaborated, so to speak, on the ego. But there were certain other beings who, during the Saturn, Sun, and Moon evolutions, had not raised themselves so far that they could take part in this organizing of the ego. They could do only what they had learned on the moon. They had to limit themselves to working on the astral body, hence there was implanted in man's astral body something that did not belong to his noblest qualities, did not come from the higher sublime beings but from the retarded intruders who had remained behind. Had these beings done this on the moon, it would have been something lofty. But through the fact that they did this on earth as stragglers, they worked into the astral body something that placed it lower than it would have been otherwise. It became endowed with instincts and passions, and with egoism. We must heed this fact that man was influenced from two sides, that he received impacts in his astral body through which the latter became debased.

Such a thing does not influence the astral body alone. Man is so constituted that the astral body transmits such an influence to the etheric body, and this again to the physical body. The astral body is active in all parts, hence these spirits work on the etheric and physical through the astral body. Had these spiritual beings not been able to exercise such an influence, something would not have appeared in man at that time. This is an enhanced selfhood in man, an increased ego-feeling. What this caused in the etheric body was all that appeared as darkening of judgment, as the possibility of error. All that the astral body accomplished in the physical body is the basis of what appeared as illness. That is the spiritual cause of illnesses in man; among animals, becoming ill is something different. We see how illness has been transplanted into man; illness is connected with the causes we have indicated here. And since the physical and etheric bodies are connected with the facts of heredity, so the priniciple of illness proceeds through the hereditary line. Let us again emphasize, however, that we must distinguish between inner illnesses and external injuries. If a man is run over, that is something entirely different. Also, certain internal illnesses can be connected with external causes; for example, if one eats something that upsets the stomach, that is something external.

Before the above-mentioned beings gained influence over man in the course of evolution, he was so organized that he reacted far more powerfully than today toward evil pressing upon him from without. But in proportion to the influence that they gained over him, he lost the instincts he had possessed for what was not right. Formerly, man's whole organization was such that he had fine instincts as to what was not right for him. Substances that are taken into the stomach today and there cause illness were then rejected simply through instinct. Gazing backward in time we come to periods when man stood in a delicate relationship to the forces of his environment, reacting sensitively to the forces in his surroundings. In this respect man grew ever less sure, less capable of rejecting what was not serviceable to him.

This is connected with something else. As man grew more inward, something occurred in the world outside; what we know as the three other kingdoms of nature arose. The three kingdoms around us arose gradually. At first, only man was present. Then the animal kingdom was added; then the plant kingdom, and finally the mineral kingdom. If we were to look back on the primeval earth when the sun was still united with it, we would find a human being in and out of whom all the substances of the physical world moved. Man still lived in the womb of the gods: everything still agreed with him, so to say. Then he had to leave behind what was precipitated as the animal kingdom. Had he carried this with him, he would not have been able to develop further. He had to expel the animal kingdom, and later the plant kingdom. What exists outside in the animals and plants is nothing other than temperaments, passions, certain traits of men that they had to expel. And when man formed his bones he expelled the mineral world. After a certain length of time, man could look upon his environment and say, "Formerly I could endure you; formerly you went in and out of me as air now does. When I still lived in the water-earth I could endure you; I digested you. Now you are outside, and I can no longer endure you, no longer digest you." As man became enclosed in his skin, as he became a self-contained separate being, he saw, in the same proportion, these kingdoms around him.

If these beings had not worked on man, something else would not have happened. As long as man is healthy, he will stand in a normal relationship to the outer world. When he has disturbed forces within him, these must be driven back by the powers that man has. If his powers are too weak for this, if he cannot provide the normal resistance, then something must be infused into him from outside. Something must be implanted into him to furnish the resistance that he still had at the time the forces from outside breathed in and out of him. It may be necessary, when a person is ill, that the forces of a metal, for example, should be injected into him. It is because man was in connection with metals earlier, in connection with plant juices and similar things, that we are justified in applying them as medicaments.

When the Egyptian initiates could look back over the whole course of world evolution, they knew precisely how the individual organs of the human body corresponded with the substances of the external world. They knew which plants and which metals had to be administered to the patient. A great treasure of occult wisdom in the domain of medicine will be raised to light one day, wisdom that mankind formerly possessed. Not only are many things bungled in medicine today, but often special healing powers are ascribed to this or that in a one-sided way. The true occultist will never be one-sided. How often must we reject efforts that would make a compromise with the science of the spirit! The latter cannot support a one-sided method: on the contrary, it seeks to establish diversified research. It is one-sided to say, "Away with all poisons!" People who say this do not know the true healing forces. Naturally many stupid things are done today, for the professionals in most cases cannot grasp all the relationships, and a certain tyranny in medical science excludes what can proceed from occultism. If there were no campaigns against the oldest methods of medicine, against the injection of metals, there could be a reform. With modern experimentation nothing is discovered that can hold its own against the traditional remedies, which only a lay ignorance can oppose as strongly as is often done. The ancient Egyptian initiates excelled in these secrets. They had an insight into the real relationships of evolution, and if today certain physicians speak in a condescending way of Egyptian medicine, you can soon tell from their tone that they know nothing about it. Here we touch upon something in the Egyptian initiation that should be known.

It was such things as these that went over into the folk-consciousness. Now we must reflect that the same souls that are in our bodies today were also incarnated in that ancient time. Let us remember that these souls saw all the images that the initiates made of what they knew through vision in the spiritual world. We know that what a soul takes into itself from incarnation to incarnation, ever and again bears fruits in one or another way. Even though man cannot remember it, it is still true that what lives in the soul today lives in it because it was deposited there earlier. The soul is formed both within and beyond the physical life. When it was between birth and death, when it was between death and a new birth, Egyptian ideas were influential and modern ideas have proceeded from these. Today certain definite ideas are developing out of the Egyptian ideas. What is called Darwinism today did not arise because of external reasons. We are the same souls who, in Egypt, received the pictures of the animal forms of man's forebears. The old views have awakened again, but man has descended more deeply into the material world. He remembers that it was said to him, "Our ancestors were animal forms." But he does not remember that these forms were gods. This is the psychological basis for the emergence of Darwinism. The figures of the gods appear in materialistic form. Thus there is an intimate spiritual connection between the old and the new, between the third and the fifth cultural periods.

Now it is not the whole destiny of our time that man should see in material form what previously he saw in the spiritual. That would have been our fate had not the Christ-impulse entered into human evolution in the meantime. This was not significant only for life on the physical plane. Today we shall see what significance the events of Palestine had for the other side of life, where the souls of the Egyptians sojourned after death. Here on the physical plane occurred the things we have already discussed. But the three years of Christ's activity, like the event of Golgotha and the baptism in Jordan, were of significance equally to the souls incarnated on earth and to those who were in the condition between death and a new birth.

Let us recall the fact that the external physical expression for the ego is the blood. What works physically in the forces of the blood is the physical expression of the ego. In the course of evolution too strong a measure of egoism made its appearance, which means that the egohood impressed the blood too powerfully. This "surplus" of egoism had to be expelled again if spirituality was to be restored to mankind. On Golgotha the impulse was given for this expulsion of egoism. In the same moment when the Redeemer's blood flowed on Golgotha, still other events were taking place in the spiritual world. The Redeemer's blood flowed out in the material world, while the superfluity of egoism passed over into the spiritual world. The superfluous egoism had to vanish from the world, and the impulse for this was given on Golgotha. In place of egoism, universal human love entered into mankind.

But what was this event of Golgotha? What was this event of a three-and-a-half-day death on the physical plane? It was the enactment on the physical plane of what also had been experienced in spiritual development by one who was initiated. He was dead for three and a half days. One who had gone through this symbolical death could say to mankind, "There is a conquering of death. There is something eternal in the world." Death was conquered by the initiates, and they felt themselves to be victors over death. The event of Golgotha signifies that what had often taken place in the mysteries of ancient times became, for once, an historical event: the conquering of death through the spirit. This was taken out into the world on the physical plane. If we let this work upon our souls, we sense what happened with the Mystery of Golgotha as something new, but also as an image of the ancient initiation. We feel this unique event entering into the world historically.

What was the consequence of this? What could the initiate do? Out of his own experiences he could say to his fellow men, "I know there is a spiritual world, that man can live in the spiritual world. I have lived in it for three and a half days and bring you tidings thence. I bring you the gifts of the spiritual world." These gifts were useful and healing to mankind.

On the other hand, one who had lived as an initiate in the physical world could bring nothing similar to the dead. To the dead he could only say, "All that happens on the physical plane is so ordered that man ought to be redeemed." Thus it was when, in the spiritual world, the ancient initiates held converse with the dead, to whom they could give only the teaching that "Life is suffering; only redemption will bring healing." Thus did Buddha still teach. Thus did the initiate teach both the living and the dead. But through the event of Golgotha death was conquered in the physical world, and this signified something for those who had died and were in the spiritual world. Those who take up Christ in their innermost parts illuminate again their shadowy life in devachan. The more man experiences here of the Christ, the brighter it becomes over there in the spiritual world. After the blood had flowed from the wounds of the Redeemer—this is something that belongs to the mysteries of Christianity—the Christ-spirit descended to the dead. This is one of the deepest mysteries of mankind. Christ descended to the dead and said to them, "Over there something has happened, of which it cannot be said that what happens there is not so important as what happens here. What man brings with him into the spiritual realm as a consequence of this event is a gift that can be brought out of the physical world into the spiritual world." These are the tidings that Christ brought to the dead in the three and a half days. He descended to the dead in order to redeem them.

In the ancient initiation one could say that the fruits of the spiritual were reaped in the physical. Now an event occurred in the physical world that produced its fruits and did its work in the spiritual world. One can say that it was not in vain that man completed his descent to the physical plane. He completed it so that here in the physical world fruits could be produced for the spiritual world.

That these fruits could be produced came to pass through Christ, who was present among the living and among the dead, who gave an impulse so intense and so powerful that it shook the whole world.

LECTURE 12

The Christ Impulse as Conqueror of Matter.

September 14, 1908

IN order to complete the task that we have envisioned, we must now study the character of our own time in the same sense in which we have studied the four post-Atlantean epochs up to the appearance of Christianity. We have seen how, after the Atlantean catastrophe, there evolved the ancient Indian epoch, the ancient Persian epoch, and the Egypto-Chaldean epoch. In the description of the fourth epoch, the Greco-Latin, we have seen that in a certain connection man at that time worked his way into the physical plane and that this working into the physical world then reached its low point. Why is this time, which from one side we call the low point of human evolution, nevertheless so attractive, so sympathetic, for the modern observer? Because this low point became the point of departure for many significant events of the present cultural epoch. We have seen how, in this Greco-Latin culture, a marriage was achieved between spirit and matter in Greek art. We have seen how the Greek temple was a building where the god could dwell, and that man could say, "I have brought matter so far that for me it can be an expression of the spirit, so that in every detail I can feel something of this spirit." Thus it is with all Greek works of art. Thus it is with everything we have to say about the life of the Greeks. This world of artistic creations, into which the spirit was implanted, made matter so terribly attractive that among us in Middle Europe the great Goethe, in his *Faust* tragedy, sought to portray his own union with this epoch of culture.

If in the succeeding time the progress of culture had continued in the same direction, what would have been the result? We can make this clear through a simple sketch. In the Greco-Latin time man had descended to his lowest point, but in such a way that in no piece of matter was the spirit lost to him. In all the creations of this time, the spirit was incorporated in matter. When we look at the figure of a Greek god, we see everywhere how the Greek creative genius imprinted the spiritual on the external matter. The Greek had conquered matter, but the spirit had not been lost. The normal course of culture would have been that man should descend below this level, plunging down below matter so that the spirit would become the slave of matter. We need only turn an unprejudiced glance on our environment and we shall see that, on one side, this has actually happened. The expression of this descent is materialism. True, in no period has man mastered matter more than in our time, but only for the satisfaction of bodily needs. We need only consider with what primitive means the gigantic pyramids were built, and then compare this with the boldness and loftiness with which the Egyptian spirit moved among the mysteries of world-existence. We need only think of the deep sense in which, for the Egyptians, their pictures of the gods were images of what took place in the cosmos and on earth in the remote past. One who, at that time in Egypt, could look into the spiritual world, lived in something that became invisible in the Atlantean time but was a fact of evolution in the Lemurian time. One who was not an initiate, who belonged to the common people, could still participate in these spiritual worlds with his whole feeling and his whole soul. Yet how primitive were the means with which these men had to work externally on the physical plane. Compare this with our own time. We need only read the innumerable eulogies that our contemporaries write about the enormous strides made in modern times. The science of the spirit makes no objection to this. Human achievements are increasing through the conquest of the elements. But let us look at the thing from another side.

Let us look back to far-distant times when men ground their corn between simple stones, yet could look up into tremendous heights of the spiritual life. The majority of men today have no inkling of the heights that were surveyed at that time. They have no inkling of what a Chaldean initiate experienced when, in his special manner, he saw the stars, animals, plants, and minerals in connection with man, when he recognized the healing forces. The Egyptian priests were men to whom the physicians of today could not hold a candle. The men of today cannot penetrate into these heights of the spiritual world. Only through the science of the spirit can an idea be formed of what the ancient Chaldean-Egyptian initiates saw. For example, what we are offered today by way of interpretation of the inscriptions, in which deep mysteries are contained, is only a caricature of the ancient significance. Thus we find that in ancient times man had little power over the tools and equipment for labor on the physical plane, but he had enormous forces in relation to the spiritual world.

Man is descending ever more deeply into matter, and more and more he devotes his spiritual powers to conquering the physical plane. Can we not say that the human spirit is becoming the slave of the physical plane? In a certain way man descends even below the physical plane. Man has devoted enormous spiritual force to inventing the steamship, the railway, and the telephone, but what does he use these for? What a mass of spirit is thus diverted from life for the higher worlds. The spiritual scientist understands this and does not criticize in our time, because he knows that it was necessary to conquer the physical plane. Yet it is true that the spirit has plunged down into the physical world. Is it important for the spirit that, instead of grinding our own corn in a quern, we should be able to call Hamburg by long-distance telephone and order what we want to be sent from America by steamer? Great spiritual force has been applied to building up such connections with America and many other foreign lands, but we may ask whether the aim of all this is not the satisfaction of the material life, of our bodily needs. Since everything in the world is limited, there is not much spiritual force left over whereby man may ascend to the spiritual world after he has devoted so much to the material. The spirit has become the slave of matter. The Greek incorporated the spirit in his works of art, but today the spirit has descended very far. We have proof of this in the many technical and mechanical arrangements of our industry, which serve only material needs. Now let us ask whether this process is completed and whether man has descended too far.

This would have been the case were it not for the occurrence that we discussed in the preceding lectures. At the low point of human evolution something was infused into mankind, through the Christ-impulse, that gave the stimulus to a new ascent. The entry of the Christ-impulse into human evolution forms the other side of culture thereafter. It showed the way to the overcoming of matter. It brought the force through which death can be overcome. Thereby it offered to humanity the possibility of again raising itself above the level of the physical plane. This mightiest impulse had to be given, this impulse which became so efficacious that matter could be overcome in the magnificent way that is described in the Gospel of John, in the Baptism in Jordan and the Mystery of Golgotha.

Christ Jesus, who was foretold by the prophets, gave the most powerful impulse of all human evolution. Man had to separate himself from the spiritual worlds in order to attach himself to them again with the Christ-being. But we cannot yet understand this if we do not penetrate still more deeply into the connections of human evolution as a whole.

We must point out that what we call the advent of the Christ on earth is an event that could occur only at the low point, when man had sunk so far. The Greco-Latin period stands in the middle of the seven post-Atlantean epochs. No other period would have been the right one. When man became a personality, God also had to become a personality in order to save him, to give him the possibility of rising again. We have seen that in his Roman citizenship the Roman first became conscious of his personality. Earlier, man still lived in the heights of the spiritual world; now he had descended entirely to the physical plane, and now he had to be led upward again through God himself. We must go more deeply into the third, the fifth, and the intermediate period. We shall not study Egyptian mythology in an academic way, but we must pick out the characteristic points in order to get deeper into the feeling-life of the ancient Egyptians. Then we may ask how this illuminates our own time. There is one thing here that must be weighed carefully.

We have seen how, in the Egyptian myths and mysteries, all the mighty pictures of the Sphinx, of Isis, of Osiris, were memories of ancient human conditions. All this was like a reflection of ancient events on earth. Man looked back into his primeval past and saw his origin. The initiate could experience again the spiritual existence of his forebears. We have seen how man grew out of an original group-soul condition. We could point out how these group-souls were preserved in the forms of the four apocalyptic beasts. Man grew out of this condition in such a way that he gradually refined his body and achieved the development of individuality. We can follow this historically. Let us read the *Germania* of Tacitus.* In the times described there, in the condi-

---

* The passage referred to is probably the following (pages 293 and 295 in the Loeb Classical Library Edition): "Sisters' children mean as much to their uncle as to their father; some tribes regard this blood-tie as even closer and more sacred than that between son and father . . . The more relations a man has and the larger the number of his connections by marriage, the more influence has he in his age; it does not pay to have no ties. It is incumbent to take up a father's feuds or a kinsman's not less than his friendship."

tions of the Germanic regions in the first century after Christ as there portrayed, we see how the consciousness of the individual is still bound up with the community, how the clan spirit rules, how the Cherusker, for example, still feels himself as a member of his clan. This consciousness is still so strong that the individual seeks vengeance for another of the same group. It finds expression in the custom of the blood-feud. Thus a sort of group-soul condition prevailed. This condition was preserved into late post-Atlantean times, but only as an echo. In the last period of Atlantis the group-consciousness generally died out. It is only stragglers whom we have just described. In reality the men of that time no longer knew anything of the group-soul. In the Atlantean time, however, man did know of it. Then he did not yet say *I* of himself. This group-soul feeling changed into something else in the following generations.

Strange as it may seem, in ancient times memory had an entirely different meaning and power. What is memory today? Reflect on whether you can still recall the events of your earliest childhood. Probably you can remember very little, and beyond your childhood you cannot go at all. You will remember nothing of what lies before your birth. It was not like this in Atlantean times. Even in the first post-Atlantean time man could remember what his father, grandfather, and ancestors had experienced. There was no sense in saying that between birth and death there was an ego. The ego reached back for centuries in the memory. The ego reached as far as the blood flowed down, from the remotest ancestors to the descendants. At that time the group-ego was not to be thought of as extended in space over the contemporaries, but as proceeding upward in the generations. Therefore, the modern man will never understand what appears as an echo of this in the tales of the patriarchs: that Adam, Noah, and others grew to be so old. They counted their ancestors through several generations upward to their ego. The modern man no longer can form any conception of this. In those days there would have been no sense in giving a single man a name between birth and death. In the whole series of ancestors the memory continued upwards for centuries. As far as man could remember through the centuries, so far was he given his name. Adam was, so to say, the ego that flowed with the blood through the generations. Only when we are acquainted with these actual facts do we know how things really were. Man felt sheltered in this series of generations. This is what the Bible means when it says, "I and Father Abraham are one." When the adherent of the Old Testament said this, only then did he rightly feel himself as man within the line of ancestry. Among the first post-Atlanteans, even among the Egyptians, this consciousness was still present. Men felt the community of the blood, and this caused something special for the spiritual life.

When a man dies today he has a life in kamaloka, after which comes a relatively long life in devachan. But this is already a result of the Christ-impulse. This was not the case in pre-Christian times; then a man felt himself connected with the times of his forefathers. Today a man must wean himself in kamaloka from the wishes and desires to which he has accustomed himself in the physical world; the duration of this condition depends upon this. We cling to our life between birth and death; in ancient times man clung to much more than this. Man was connected with the physical plane in such a way that he felt himself as a member of the whole physical series of generations. Thus, in kamaloka, one did not merely have to work out the clinging to an individual physical existence, but one really had to traverse all that was connected with the generations, up to the remotest ancestor. One experienced this backwards. One result of this was the deep truth underlying the expression: "To feel oneself sheltered in Abraham's bosom." One felt that after death he went upward through the whole row of ancestors, and the road that one had to travel was called "the way to the fathers." Only when one had traversed this path could he ascend into the spiritual worlds and travel the way of the gods. At that time the soul traveled first the path of the fathers and then the path of the gods.

Now the various cultures did not come to abrupt ends. The

essence of the Indian culture remained, although it underwent a change. It was preserved alongside the following cultures. In the continuation of the Indian culture that was contemporaneous with the Egyptian, something similar arose. Today we easily confuse what was later with what was earlier. Therefore it was emphasized that I was giving indications only out of the remotest periods. Among other things, the Indians now took up the view of the path of the fathers and the path of the gods.

As a man became more initiated, freed himself more from dependence on home and the fathers, became more homeless, the path of the gods became longer and the path of the fathers became shorter. One who clung closely to the fathers had a long father-path and a short god-path. In the terminology of the Orient, the way of the fathers was called *Pitriyana* and the way of the gods was called *Devayana*. When we speak of devachan, we should understand that this is only a distorted form of the word *Devayana*, the path of the gods. An old Vedantist would simply laugh at us if we came to him with descriptions such as we give of devachan. It is not so easy to find one's way into the oriental methods of thinking and contemplating. As to those who pretend to give out oriental truths, these truths often must be protected from just such people. Many a person today who accepts something as Indian teaching has no idea that he is receiving a confused doctrine. The modern science of the spirit does not claim to be an oriental-Indian teaching. In certain circles people love what comes from far away, perhaps from America, but the truth is at home everywhere. Antiquarian research belongs to scholars, but the science of the spirit is life. Its truth can be checked everywhere at any time. We must keep this before our minds.

What we have just mentioned was practice as well as theory among the ancient Egyptians. What was taught in the great mysteries was also practical. Something special was connected with this, as we shall learn as we penetrate further. The mysteries of the ancient Egyptians strove for something special. Today we may smile when we are told how the Pharaoh was at a certain time a kind of initiate, and how the Egyptian stood in relation to the Pharaoh and to his state institutions. For the modern European scholar it is particularly comical when the Pharaoh gives himself the name, "Son of Horus," or even "Horus." It seems singular to us that a man should be venerated as a god; nothing more abstruse could be thought of. But the man of today does not understand the Pharaoh and his mission. He does not know what the Pharaoh-initiation really was. Today we see in a people, only a group of persons who can be counted. To the man of today a people* is a meaningless abstraction. The reality is simply a certain number of persons filling a certain area. But this is not a people for one who accepts the standpoint of occultism.** As a single member such as the finger belongs to the whole body, so do the single persons within the people belong to the folk-soul. They are as it were embedded in it, but the folk-soul is not physical; it is real only as an etheric form. It is an absolute reality; the initiate can commune with this soul. It is even much more real for him than are single individualities among the people, far more so than a single person. For the occultist spiritual experiences are entirely valid, and there the folk-soul is something thoroughly real. Let us examine briefly the connection between the folk-soul and the individuals.

If we think of the single individuals, the single egos, as little circles, for external physical observation they will be separate beings. But one who observes these single individualities spiritually sees them as though embedded in an etheric cloud, and this is the incorporation of the folk-soul. If the single person thinks, feels, and wills something, he radiates his feelings and thoughts into the common folk-soul. This is colored by his radiations, and the folk-soul becomes permeated by the thoughts and feelings of the single persons. When we look away from the physical man and observe only his etheric and astral bodies, and

* The German word *Volk* has no convenient English equivalent. We shall translate it as *people* or *folk* in different contexts.
** Rudolf Steiner's fullest discussion of this subject appears in his cycle of lectures, *Mission of the Folk-Souls*, delivered at Oslo in 1910.

then observe the astral body of an entire people, we see that the astral body of the entire people receives its color-shadings from the single persons.

The Egyptian initiate knew this, but he also knew something further. When he observed this folk-substance, the ancient Egyptian asked himself what really lived in the folk-soul. What did he see therein? He saw in his folk-soul the reembodiment of Isis. He saw how she had once wandered among men. Isis worked in the folk-soul. He saw in her the same influences as those that proceeded from the moon; these forces worked in the folk-soul. What the Egyptian saw as Osiris worked in the individual spiritual radiations; therein he recognized the Osiris-influence. But Isis he saw in the folk-soul.

Thus Osiris was not visible on the physical plane. He had died for the physical plane. Only when a man had died was Osiris again placed before his eyes. Therefore we read in the *Book of the Dead* how the Egyptian felt that he was united with Osiris in death, that he himself became an Osiris. Osiris and Isis worked together in the state and in the single person, as his members.

Now let us again consider the Pharaoh, remembering that this was a reality for him. Each Pharaoh received certain instructions before his initiation, to the end that he should not grasp this with his intellect only, but that it should become truth and reality for him. He had to be brought to the point where he could say to himself, "If I am to rule this people, I must sacrifice a portion of my spirituality, I must extinguish a part of my astral and etheric bodies. The Osiris and Isis principles must work in me. I must will nothing personally; if I say something, Osiris must speak; if I do something, Osiris must do it; if I move my hand, Osiris and Isis must be active. I must represent Horus, the son of Isis and Osiris."

Initiation is not erudition. But to be able to do something like this, to be able to make such a sacrifice, pertains to initiation. What the Pharaoh sacrificed of himself could be filled up with portions of the folk-soul. The part of himself that the Pharaoh relinquished was just what gave him power. For justified power does not arise through a man's raising his own personality; it arises through his taking into himself something that transcends the boundaries of personality, a higher spiritual power. The Pharaoh took such a power into himself, and this was externally portrayed through the Uraeus-serpent.

Again we have peered into a mystery. We have seen something much higher than the explanations that are given today when the Pharaohs are discussed.

If the Egyptian cherished such feelings, what would have to be his particular concern? It would be his particular concern that the folk-soul should become as strong as possible, rich in good forces, and that it should not be diminished. The Egyptian initiates could not reckon with what man possessed through blood-relationship. But what the forefathers had accumulated as spiritual riches, was to become the property of the individual soul. This is indicated for us in the judging of the dead, where the man is brought before the forty-two assessors of the dead. There his deeds are weighed. Who are the forty-two judges of the dead? They are the ancestors.* It was believed that each man's life was interwoven with the lives of forty-two ancestors. Therefore he had to answer to them as to whether he actually had taken up what they had offered to him spiritually. In this way, what was contained in the Egyptian mystery-teachings was something that was to become practical for life, but which could also be turned to good account for the time beyond death, for the life between death and a new birth. In the Egyptian epoch man was already entangled in the physical world. But at the same time he had to look up to his ancestors in the other world, and cultivate in the physical world what he had inherited from them. Through this interest he was fettered to the physical plane, since he had to continue working on what his fathers had created.

Now we must reflect that the souls of today are reincarnations of the ancient Egyptian souls. For the souls of today, who

---

* A full description of these 42 gods is to be found in Budge, *Osiris and the Egyptian Resurrection,* Volume I, pp. 316–317. For a fairly good picture, see pages 344–45 of the same work.

experienced it in their Egyptian incarnation, what is the significance of what happened at that time? All that the soul experienced at that time between death and a new birth has been woven into the soul, weaves within it, and has arisen again in our fifth period, which brings the fruits of the third period. These fruits appear in the inclinations and ideas of modern times, which have their causes in the ancient Egyptian world. Nowadays all the ideas emerge which at that time were laid down in the soul as germs. Therefore it is easy to see that man's modern conquests on the physical plane are nothing more than a coarser version of the transfer of interest to the physical plane that was present in ancient Egypt, only people are now even more deeply ensnared in matter. In the mummifying of the dead we have already seen a cause of the materialistic views that we now experience on the physical plane.

Let us imagine a soul of that time. Let us imagine a soul that then lived as a pupil of one of the ancient initiates. Such a pupil's spiritual gaze had been directed to the cosmos through actual perception. The way Osiris and Isis lived in the moon had become spiritual perception for him. Everything was permeated by divine-spiritual beings. He had taken this into his soul. He is again incarnated in the fourth and fifth periods. In the fifth period such a person experiences all this again. It comes back to him as a memory. What happens to it now? The pupil had gazed up at all that lived in the world of the stars. This sight comes to life again in a certain person of the fifth period. He remembers what he saw and heard at that time. He cannot recognize it again, because it has taken on a material coloring. It is no longer the spiritual that he sees, but the material-mechanical relationships emerge again and he recreates the thoughts in materialistic form as memory. Where he had previously seen divine beings, Isis and Osiris, now he sees only abstract forces without any spiritual bond. The spiritual relationships appear to him in thought-form. Everything arises again, but in material form.

Let us apply this to a particular soul which at that time

acquired insight into the great cosmic connections, and let us imagine that there arises again before this soul what it had seen spiritually in ancient Egypt. This appears again in this soul in the fifth post-Atlantean period, and we have the soul of Copernicus. Thus did the Copernican system arise, as a memory-tableau of spiritual experiences in ancient Egypt. The case is the same with Kepler's system. These men gave birth to their great laws out of their memories, out of what they had experienced in the Egyptian time. Now let us think how such a thing arises in the soul as a faint memory, and let us think also how what such a spirit truly thinks was, in ancient Egypt, experienced by him in spiritual form. What can such a spirit say to us? That it seems to him as though he looked back into ancient Egypt. It is as though he stated all this in a new form when such a spirit says, "But now, a year and a half after the first dawning, a few months after the first full daylight, a few weeks after the pure sun had risen over these most wonderful contemplations, nothing holds me back any longer. I shall revel in holy fire. I shall scorn the sons of men with the simple confession that I am stealing the sacred vessels of the Egyptians to build with them an habitation for my God, far removed from the borders of Egypt." Is this not like an actual memory, which corresponds to the truth? This is Kepler's saying, and in his works we also find the following: "The ancient memory is knocking at my heart." Wonderful are the connections of things in human evolution. Many such enigmatic sayings take on light and meaning when one senses the spiritual connections. Life becomes great and powerful, and we feel our way into a mighty whole when we understand that the single person is only an individual form of the spiritual that permeates the world.

I have already pointed out that what has arisen in our time as Darwinism is a coarser materialistic version of what the Egyptians portrayed as their gods in animal form. I was also able to show that if one understands Paracelsus correctly, his medical lore is a recrudescence of what was taught in the temples of ancient Egypt. Let us contemplate such a spirit as Paracelsus.

We find a remarkable statement by him. One who has steeped himself in Paracelsus knows what a lofty spirit lived in him. He made a remarkable statement, saying that he had learned much in many ways; least of all in the academies, but much from old traditions and from the common people during his journeys through many lands. It is impossible here to give examples of the deep truths that are still present among the common people but are no longer understood, although Paracelsus could still turn them to account. He said that he had found one book containing deep medical truths. What book was it? The Bible! Thereby he meant not only the Old Testament, but also the New. One need only be able to read the Bible to find therein what Paracelsus found. What became of the medicine of Paracelsus? It is true that it is a memory of the ancient Egyptian methods of healing. But through the fact that he absorbed the mysteries of Christianity, the upward impulse, his works are saturated with spiritual wisdom, they are filled with Christ. This is the path into the future. This is what everyone must do who, in modern times, will pave the way back out of the fall into matter. We must not undervalue the great material progress, but there is also the possibility of letting the spiritual flow into it.

One who studies what material science can offer today, who plunges into material science and is not too lazy to steep himself in it, such a man acts wisely also in relation to the science of the spirit. Much can be learned from the purely materialistic investigators. What is found there we can permeate with the pure spirit, which the science of the spirit offers. If thus we permeate everything with the spiritual, then this is properly understood Christianity. It is a slander of the science of the spirit when men say that it is is a fantastic view of the world. It can stand firmly on the ground of reality, and it would be only a most elementary beginning in the science of the spirit if one were to concentrate on a schematic representation of the higher worlds. It is not important that the student should simply know the things, learning the concepts by heart. This is not all that counts. The important thing is that the teachings about the higher worlds should become fruitful in men, that the true spiritual-scientific teachings should be introduced into everything, into the everyday life.

It is not so important that one should preach about universal brotherly love. It is best to speak of that as little as possible. Speaking in such phrases is like saying to the stove, "Dear stove, it is your duty to warm this room. Fulfill your duty!" So it is with teachings that are given through such phrases. The important thing is the means. The stove remains cold if I simply tell it that it should be warm. It gets warm when it has fuel. People also remain cold when they are admonished. But what is fuel for the modern man? The specific facts of spiritual teaching are fuel for man.* One should not be so lazy as to remain content with "Universal brotherhood." People must be given fuel. Then brotherhood will arise of itself. As the plants stretch out their blossoms to the sun, so must we all look up to the sun of the spiritual life.

The important thing is that the matters we have examined here should not be accepted merely as theoretical doctrines, but that they should become a force in our souls. For every man, in every position in practical life, they can give impulses for what he must create. People who look today at the science of the spirit with a certain scorn feel themselves superior to its "fantastic" teachings. They find "unprovable assertions" therein and say that one should cleave to the facts. If the spiritual scientist were made pusillanimous rather than bold through his life in the science of the spirit, it would be easy for him to lose his sureness and energy when he sees how just those persons who should understand the science of the spirit are the ones who utterly fail to grasp it.

Our times easily look down on what the Egyptians recognized as their gods. The latter are said to be meaningless abstractions. But modern man is far more superstitious. He clings to entirely

* This thought is more fully expounded in Rudolf Steiner's booklet, *Anthroposophical Ethics,* comprising three lectures delivered in 1912 in Norrköping.

different gods, who are authorities for him. Because he does not actually bend the knee before them, he does not notice what superstitions he cherishes.

My dear friends, when we have thus been together again we should always be mindful that when we disperse we should not take with us only a number of truths, but we should take away a collective impression, a feeling, that can properly take the form of an impulse of will, an impulse to carry the science of the spirit into life and to allow nothing to disturb our confidence in it.

Let us place a picture before our soul. One often hears it said, "Oh, these seekers for the spirit! They assemble in their lodges and pursue all kinds of fantastic rubbish. A man of really modern views can have no part in that." The adherents of the science of the spirit sometimes seem to be a sort of pariah class, regarded as uneducated and untrained. Should we be discouraged because of this? No. We shall place a picture before our souls and arouse the feelings that are connected with it. We can recall something similar in past times; how something similar occurred in ancient Rome. We can see how, in ancient Rome, primitive Christianity spread among a despised class of people. We look with legitimate delight today on such things as the Colosseum constructed by imperial Rome. But we can also look at the people who then regarded themselves as the choicest of their time; we can see how they sat in the Circus and watched while the Christians were burned in the arena and incense was kindled to quench the stink of the burning bodies.

Now let us look at those despised ones. They lived in the catacombs, in underground passages. There the spreading Christianity had to hide. There they erected the first Christian altars on the graves of their dead. There below they had their wonderful symbols and shrines. A strange feeling seizes us today when we walk through the catacombs, through that despised underground Rome. The Christians knew what awaited them. That first germ of the Christ-impulse on earth, confined to the catacombs, was despised. But what remains of imperial Rome?

150

It has disappeared from the earth, while what then lived in the catacombs has been exalted.

Let us hope that those who today wish to make themselves the bearers of a spiritual world-view may preserve the confidence of the first Christians. The representatives of the science of the spirit may be despised by contemporary academic learning, but they know that they are working for what will bloom and thrive in the future. Let them learn to endure all the vexations of the present day. We are working into the future. This we may feel confidently and without arrogance, firm against the misunderstandings of our time.

With such feelings let us try to give permanence to what has passed before our souls. Let us take it away with us as force, and let us continue to work together fraternally in the right direction.